Descriptive Metadata for Television

Descriptive Metadata for Television
An End-to-End Introduction

Mike Cox
Linda Tadic
Ellen Mulder

Focal Press
Taylor & Francis Group

NEW YORK AND LONDON

First published 2006

This edition published 2013
by Focal Press
70 Blanchard Road, Suite 402, Burlington, MA 01803

Simultaneously published in the UK
by Focal Press
2 Park Square, Milton Park, Abingdon, Oxon OX14 4RN

Focal Press is an imprint of the Taylor & Francis Group, an informa business

Notices

Practitioners and researchers must always rely on their own experience and knowledge
in evaluating and using any information, methods, compounds, or experiments described
herein. In using such information or methods they should be mindful of their own safety
and the safety of others, including parties for whom they have a professional responsibility.

To the fullest extent of the law, neither the Publisher nor the authors, contributors, or
editors, assume any liability for any injury and/or damage to persons or property as a matter
of products liability, negligence or otherwise, or from any use or operation of any methods,
products, instructions, or ideas contained in the material herein.

Library of Congress Cataloging-in-Publication Data
Cox, Michael (Michael Edward), 1945–
    Descriptive metadata for television : an end-to-end introduction / Michael Cox,
Ellen Mulder, Linda Tadic.
        p.   cm.
    Includes index.
    ISBN-13: 978-0-240-80730-0 (pbk. : alk. paper)
    ISBN-10: 0-240-80730-8 (pbk. : alk. paper)
     1. Metadata.   2. Information storage and retrieval systems—Television programs.
    3. Cataloging of audio-visual materials—Standards.   I. Mulder, Ellen.   II. Tadic, Linda.
    III. Title.
    Z666.7C69 2006
    025.3—dc22

                                                                            2005033795

British Library Cataloguing-in-Publication Data
A catalogue record for this book is available from the British Library.

ISBN 13: 978-0-240-80730-0 (pbk)

Contents

Introduction   x

1 What Is Metadata?   1
   So, What *Is* "Metadata"?   2
   What Metadata Is Not: Myths and Facts   2
   Perceptions of Metadata   3
   Relationships with Current and Future Broadcast Technologies   4
   The Perceived Relationship with the Data Handling (Information)
      Technologies   5
   The Very Real Relationship with Information Science   6
   Data Structures, Rules, and Values   7
      Data Structure or Schema   8
      Data Rules   8
      Data Values   9
   Metadata as the Key to Knowledge Management during the
      Production Processes   10
   Knowing What You've Got and Everything about It   10
   Libraries as a Resource and Gold Mine   11
      Film Studios   11
      Broadcast News   12
      Broadcast Entertainment   12
      The TV-Anytime Concept for the Use of Libraries   13
   Where *Is* the Metadata?   14
   Metadata Synchronization   18

2   **Types of Metadata**   19
    The "Purpose" of Metadata   19
      Descriptive   19
      Administrative   21
      Preservation   21
    Metadata in the Workflow   22
      The Metadata of Program Production and Publication   22
      Metadata Flow   29
      The Metadata of Program Publication and Consumption   30

3   **Metadata Schemes, Structures, and Encoding**   37
    Metadata Schemes and Structures   37
    Object Records and Item Records (Complex Objects)   40
    Metadata Structure Standards   41
      Broadcast Industry Standards   41
        Society of Motion Picture and Television Engineers   41
        European Broadcasting Union P/Meta   43
        Institut für Rundfunktechnik GmbH (IRT)   44
        Motion Picture Experts Group MPEG-7   44
        Motion Picture Experts Group MPEG-21   47
        Corporation for Public Broadcasting PBCore   49
        British Broadcasting Corporation Standard Media Exchange
          Framework (SMEF)   50
      Press Industry Standard   50
        International Press Telecommunications Council (IPTC)
          NewsML   50
      Library Standards   50
        Dublin Core Metadata Initiative   50
        Library of Congress MARC 21   51
      Archival Standards   52
        International Federation of Television Archives (FIAT/IFTA)   52
        Independent Media Arts Preservation (IMAP)   52
    Metadata Rules Standards   53
      Anglo-American Cataloguing Rules (AACR2)   53
      Archival Moving Image Materials, Version 2 (AMIM2)   54
    Metadata Value Standards   54
      Using Controlled Vocabularies and Thesauri   54
        International Press Telecommunications Council (IPTC)   55
        Library of Congress Name Authority File (LCNAF)   56
        Library of Congress Subject Headings (LCSH)   57
        Moving Image Genre-Form Guide   57
    Maintenance of Metadata   58
    Encoding of Metadata   59

4   **The Impact of Technology Change on People and
    Metadata Processes**   61
    How Is Metadata Captured and Stored?   64
    Who Owns the Metadata?   67
      Workflow Ownership   67
      Legal Information and Metadata Content Ownership   68
        Legal Information   68
        Legal Ownership of the Metadata   69
      Business Ownership   69
    Practicalities and Opportunities of Desktop Production in the
      New Workflows   70
    Where Can Metadata Leak Away?   72
    Authenticity in Metadata   73
    Mapping Metadata to Different Systems   74

5   **Identifiers and Identification**   76
    Registered Identifiers   78
      International Registration Authorities   78
      Identifiers with Program Production Relevance   81
        International Standards Organisation   81
        Society of Motion Picture and Television Engineers
          Registration Authority (SMPTE-RA)   81
        International Digital Object Identifier (DOI) Foundation   82
        Institution of Electrical & Electronic Engineers (IEEE)   82
        European Broadcasting Union (EBU)   83
        Internet Engineering Task Force (IETF)   83
      Summary: Registered Identifiers   83
    Unregistered Identifiers   83
      Unique Material Identifier (UMID)   84
      Universal Unique Identifier (UUID)   85
      Summary: Unregistered Identifiers   86
    Identifiers with Production to Consumer Relevance   86
      Digital Video Broadcasting Project (DVB)   86
      Advanced Television Systems Committee (ATSC)   87
      Internet Assigned Numbers Authority (IANA)   87
      Content ID Forum (cIDF)   87
      TV-Anytime Forum (TVA)   87
      Corporation for National Research Initiatives (CNRI)   87

6   **Metadata for the Consumer**   89
    Online: Yes or No?   91
    Metadata as the Connector between Broadcast Content and
      Internet Content   93

Metadata and Consumer Needs   94
Stages of the Production and Transmission Process Chains to
  the Consumer   95
  TV-Anytime Metadata Data Model   95
    Content Creation   95
    Content Publishing   95
    Metadata Editing   95
    Metadata Aggregation   96
    Metadata Publishing   96
    Content Selection   97
    Location Resolution   97
Metadata Elements   97
  The Content Reference ID (CRID)   97
  Attractors   98
  Suggested Elements to Create Attractors   98
Metadata for Locating the "Stuff"   101
Metadata in Marketing   102
  Added Value for the Viewer   103
  Added Value for the Marketers   103
Other Useful Metadata   104
  Modification Date   104
  Audio and Video Information   104
  File Information   104

7 **Metadata in Public Collections**   106
Donations by Broadcasters   107
  Newsfilm   107
  Current Affairs Programs and Documentaries   108
Donations by Individuals and Production Companies   109
Programs Recorded Off-Air   109
Metadata Added by the Public Archive   109
  Adapting Legacy Metadata   109
  Tracking History and Provenance   110
  Preservation Metadata   110
  Intellectual Property   111
Getting Metadata out to the Public   111

Appendix 1 Sample Metadata Records   113
  PBCore   113
    Kentucky Educational Television   113
    Wisconsin Public Television   116
    Raw News Footage Cataloging: CNN   118
    CNN Library Metadata Dictionary (Field List)   120

Entertainment Program in MARC   122
Resources for Sample Metadata Records   130

Appendix 2 Extracts from SMPTE Documents   131

Index   135

Introduction

Moving image technology dates back well over a century and sound recording longer than that. It is possible today to watch clips from 19th-century wars or listen to Tennyson himself reading "The Charge of the Light Brigade." Television is the new kid on the block by comparison, with surviving recordings dating from the 1920s (recorded on shellac discs) or "high-definition" 405 line recordings from the 1930s (recorded on film). We can still find these old recordings, and we still know what they are, who made them, why, and when because they are carefully cataloged and preserved in libraries or archives. Librarians would point out that this has been their work, not just with audiovisual material but with every medium that has captured information since about the time of Alexander the Great some millennia ago. But not only librarians use this "metadata." Everyone involved in television program-making does, from the earliest idea in the production office right through to the listings agencies and, of course, the viewer.

There has always been the film can with the title written on it. There has always been the piece of paper inside the can with the film, often with a note such as "Wednesday racing clip gone to Friday 'South Today.'" There have always been camera operators writing the shot details on the film can or tape box. There have always been production staff researching and logging the film or tape that was in the can. There have always been editors making their own notes and keeping their own logs. There have always been directors assembling the program in their own minds with the help of sheets of paper stuck together, cut up, rearranged, and stuck back together again. There have always been people looking after the administration and all the paperwork it involved, and there was always the archive where program material was sent for "safekeeping." There was always the playout department, which seemed to rely solely on published listings, and there was always the viewer who did the same.

So what has suddenly changed to make "metadata" such a buzzword? To put it at its simplest, the advent of digital technology opens up the possibility, for the first time, to treat anything that can be processed by a computer in the same way— pictures, sounds, written material, and possibly things we have not yet thought of are all the same to a digital system. Because all these can now be processed digitally, why not just join up all the processes? But here is the rub—for over a century, everyone involved has been doing things differently from everybody else, so joining things up is, to use an engineering phrase, "not as simple as that" in spite of what the sales reps say! We have to look again at the processes that have developed over 100 years or more and then try to reengineer them to fit together, not so much in terms of hardware but in terms of managing the processes and the information each needs. During the next year or two, we have to reinvent a situation that it took us 100 years to get into—no mean task. Managing the processes implies a knowledge of what we have in the system and all the information about it—unambiguously, because machines are even easier to confuse than people.

So now, disciplines with different approaches and backgrounds suddenly have to work ever more closely together. They have to understand each other's techniques, the aspirations of the program makers, and the boundaries of the technology. So it was that this book came to be written.

This book is intended as an introduction for those involved operationally in making television programs or archiving and caring for the completed programs. It highlights many of the interoperability issues involved but does not attempt to solve them, only perhaps point up the questions that others will solve. It is *not* an in-depth thesis on any of the topics mentioned. Anyone working in a given discipline will probably find some parts to be too shallow, while other parts will introduce new concepts. Neither is the book exhaustive in its scope—for example, it touches only on the better known standards likely to be encountered in TV production. The hope is that everyone will learn something.

Three authors were involved, with the hope of effectively spanning the disciplines, two continents, and two and a quarter languages—so expect to see some seams. We would each like to thank the other authors for their enlightenment in attempting this book, not to mention families and friends who have had to endure its writing. Appreciation also goes to those who took the time to review the work and provide us with speedy feedback and encouragement.

1 What Is Metadata?

"That shows that there are three hundred and sixty-four days when you get un-birthday presents," said Humpty Dumpty.

"Certainly," said Alice.

"And only one *for birthday presents, you know, there's glory for you!"*

"I don't know what you mean by 'glory,'" Alice said.

Humpty Dumpty smiled contemptuously. "Of course you don't—till I tell you. I meant 'there's a nice knock-down argument for you!'"

"But 'glory' doesn't mean 'a nice knock-down argument,'" Alice objected.

"When I use a word," Humpty Dumpty said in a rather a scornful tone, *"it means just what I choose it to mean—neither more nor less."*

"The question is," said Alice, *"whether you can make words mean different things."*

"The question is," said Humpty Dumpty, *"which is to be master—that's all."*

Alice was too much puzzled to say anything, so after a minute Humpty Dumpty began again. "They've a temper, some of them—particularly verbs, they're the proudest—adjectives you can do anything with, but not verbs—however, I can manage the whole lot! Impenetrability! That's what I say!"

"Would you tell me, please," said Alice, *"what that means?"*

"Now you talk like a reasonable child," said Humpty Dumpty, looking very much pleased. *"I meant by 'impenetrability' that we've had enough of that subject, and it would be just as well if you'd mention what you meant to do next, as I suppose you don't intend to stop here all the rest of your life."*

"That's a great deal to make one word mean," Alice said in a thoughtful tone.

"When I make a word do a lot of work like that," said Humpty Dumpty, *"I always pay it extra."*

"Oh!" said Alice. She was too much puzzled to make any other remark.

—Lewis Carroll

Humpty's conversation with Alice will sound familiar to anyone who has been involved with making programs. The different disciplines involved in making programs have for many years used the same words to mean subtly different things. New technologies have brought their own words and meanings as new concepts are introduced and new ways of working become possible. A few years ago, "metadata" was a word that nobody used. Now suddenly it is everywhere, yet there is nothing new about it.

So, What *Is* "Metadata"?

The traditional answer is that the word "metadata" comes from the Greek "meta," meaning "about," so that metadata literally means "about data." To most people, this is about as helpful as Humpty's explanation to Alice. In the simplest terms, metadata is a particular detail of information about something else.

Program makers work with sights and sounds. In theater, these are real and involve working with real settings, real people, and real music with the audience physically present for the production. In television, the audience is remote and views or hears a reconstruction of the sights and sounds produced from some form of electronic representation of the original, which may or may not have been stored as a recording. In all these cases, the people in the audience will want some detail of the show if they are to be in the right place at the right time for the right show. At the least they will want to know the title of the show, how to find it, and what time it is to be performed—in other words, they will want some details about the show. They want some "metadata."

What Metadata Is Not: Myths and Facts

In spite of the current hype in the industry, metadata is not magic! Neither is it a panacea to bad practice and there is no metadata cavalry galloping over the hill to rescue us from rising costs, ever tighter budgets, union demands, bad management, deadlines, or more competition. Metadata is not a threat to the quality of programs, and it is not something that can be just bolted on by buying the latest piece of equipment. Metadata is not "digital" (whatever that means), though the word is often associated with digital hardware and applications.

Most important, metadata is meaningful information in its aggregate—a single item of metadata is merely a piece of detail data and in isolation is not usually very informative. Several items of metadata grouped together are probably necessary to convey useful information. Further, *information* is not *knowledge*—only when the right pieces of information are perceived in the correct relationship will knowledge dawn. This implies increasingly complex structures as simple metadata elements are used to convey firstly information and then knowledge. This increasing complexity is reflected in the way we use metadata—not as simple data elements alone or even in groups, but in complex structures and substructures each with their own rules.

Perceptions of Metadata

The perception of metadata is one of those curious things that depends on where you stand and where you start from. One person's important metadata is another person's rubbish. In addition, there can be several layers of metadata. For example, a written description of a program might be considered metadata—or the description itself might have its own metadata, such as the name of the person who wrote it.

Some of the edges get very blurred: a browse or preview copy of a program might arguably be considered metadata because it is a descriptive proxy for the real thing—until the original is destroyed and you have to broadcast it! Indeed the electronic representations of sights and sounds we all are used to in television might be considered to be descriptive and therefore metadata. Proxies are frequently used in program making as a research tool and usually (perhaps erroneously) referred to as browse video or browse audio—they are not a usable copy but are instead descriptive of the broadcast-quality original.

Fortunately, the industry has come up with some basic definitions to give itself a starting point. The following definitions from the Society of Motion Picture and Television Engineers (SMPTE) were derived as a consequence of the final report of the "EBU/SMPTE Task Force for Harmonised Standards for the Exchange of Programme Material as Bitstreams" published in August 1998:

Any data or signal necessary to represent any single type of visual, aural, or other sensory experience (independent of the method of coding) is **Essence**.

Any one or any combination of picture (or video) essences, sound (or audio) essences and data (or auxiliary) essences is **Material**.

That data which convey information about Material is **Metadata**.

Material in combination with any associated Metadata is **Content**.

The definition of "essence" introduces an important concept—also a difficult one because it is challenging to conceptualize essence without instinctively attaching metadata to it in one's own mind. As a result, there is often confusion between the program essence and the program content. At the same time, the word "material" is frequently used as a sort of slang term for almost anything to do with a program, with no further thought given about what the word might *really* mean.

It is important to recognize that metadata can exist before the essence about which it conveys information—for example, titles, project numbers, or shooting schedules can all fall into this category. Equally, the metadata can exist long after the essence has been destroyed, as might be the case with rushes where some of the metadata continues to have importance but the essence does not—for example, contact details or historical information.

Relationships with Current and Future Broadcasting Technologies

In traditional film- or tape-based program making, the essence as previously defined is either transmitted "live" as an electronic signal or captured onto a storage medium—either chemically on a suitable emulsion or magnetically onto magnetic particles. In these cases, a supporting plastic strip is used as a physical base for the actual storage medium to form a reel of film or tape, which is kept safe in a film tin or tape cassette along with identifying data, titles, and the like—in other words, along with basic metadata. Even a live feed will have supporting metadata about its source, title, and so on.

In the production office, project plans are drawn up, contracts issued, scripts written, and so on. All these processes produce their own metadata—but then the people involved in the work traditionally store the metadata they produced independently of each other in a variety of word processing files, spreadsheets, diaries, filofaxes, and Post-it notes.

Once the program is finished, it is passed on to the archive or library for safe keeping. Librarians will catalog and classify the content, possibly using a proxy copy, and enter the resulting informative metadata in their database so they can retrieve it in the future. However, rarely if ever is the metadata from the rest of the process passed on to them, except, perhaps, for the title, tape number, and basic technical information about recording formats. It has to be re-created, with all the associated risk of errors and lack of accuracy—not to mention the work and time involved.

As the electronic technologies of program making converge with the newer concepts and technologies made possible by the computer industry, working practices are starting to change: program material need no longer be stored on magnetic tapes but can be stored in exactly the same way as word processor or spreadsheet files—that is, literally as computer data files. Program material no longer needs to be moved from place to place by physically transporting the tape or by the use of specialized and expensive communication circuits. Many different users can work on the same program material at the same time, independently of each other.

The downside is that the old numbered tape boxes are gone. Material can be ingested into a digital, computer-based system entirely automatically, without anyone ever having seen it, and stored in some nether region of cyberspace. Files are nebulous, intangible things with no obvious way to track or find them, except by the file name—did we call it doc1.doc or clip1.avi? Is it Fredsclip2.wav or Tuesday6.bwf? 1pmmurder.mpg or pmhanging.mxf? Or did the machine give it its own number—4872bro1.abc? We know Linda was the reporter, but how does that help us now?

This is why "metadata" has become such a buzzword as new digital technologies are introduced into the workplace: it is the word the new technologies use and, while it always was important, it is becoming an increasingly crucial part of the workflow, right from its start. Applications are emerging that can automatically capture metadata such as color, texture, and sounds, or even the spoken word as text. Material increasingly has to be tightly linked to its metadata right from the beginning, at the originating camera or microphone; the relationships between the different pieces of metadata have to be preserved, and metadata has to be transported, copied, and updated as work progresses on the program. In short, the metadata has to be properly managed right from the start. In a big enterprise such as CNN or the BBC, if a piece of program gets lost inside a computer-based system, it will probably stay lost.

The Perceived Relationship with the Data Handling (Information) Technologies

Once again, this problem of managing data files is not new. Personal computers began to appear in the 1980s, and at that time little thought had been given to the problem of finding things—some of us remember the early DOS keyboard commands and the seemingly impenetrable screens and unhelpful messages they produced when all we were trying to do was to find our half-finished document:

```
0 File(s)  0 bytes
18 Dir(s)  9,047,680 bytes free
Directory of C:\Mike and Mirador
10/06/2004 21:36 <DIR> .
10/10/2004 22:00 <DIR> ..
07/09/2004 16:28 <DIR> Mike
30/09/2004 14:11 <DIR> Mirador
0 File(s)  0 bytes
4 Dir(s)  9,047,680 bytes free
C:\Mike and Mirador>mirador
'mirador' is not recognized as an internal or external
command, operable program or batch file.
F:\Mike and Mirador>cd Mirador
F:\Mike and Mirador\Mirador>
. . . and so on
```

Fortunately, the situation has improved since then, and we now work with much better tools, often graphics based, which are friendlier and easier to manage. Yet how many of us can truly say that we have never forgotten what we called a word-processing document or a spreadsheet, or lost something because of a spelling mistake?

This change has, of course, been driven by the demand from real users for tools they understand. Tools have been developed to give a pictorial view of the workings of the computer system. Because much of the demand was from people using personal computers in an office environment, office terminology was often adopted, such as "files," "directories," "folders," and "cabinets." Data was stored in binary form on cassettes or discs, which required electric motors to drive them, and the term "drive" appeared in computer language.

Finding your word-processing file has become much easier due to graphical interfaces—provided you know some simple data about the file, such as its name (or even a fragment of its name), when you stored it, which folder you stored it in, and which drive that folder is on. Most of us can manage this from memory for current work in progress or by normal office good practice in the way the filing has been structured, perhaps based on past experience. There are also simple applications to help. Search engines or book-marking systems can jog our memory as to what we named the file and some will do automatic text-based indexing. So there has come to be a perception that finding word-processing documents in a computer is the same as finding TV program files in the TV archive. In practice, however, and particularly for *older* files or when you are looking for *someone else's files*, it has much in common with trying to find a needle in a haystack or maybe a book in a large public library. Some sort of properly structured and managed knowledge-based indexing system is needed. The importance of this is clear in many broadcast archives where collections contain several millions of hours of program content dating, in some cases, back to the 19th century (due to the inheritance of news film footage and early broadcast sound recordings). Media in these collections include wax cylinder or wire recordings, film footage from Victorian times, extensive European footage of World War I, and many samples of privately shot material. No mean haystack in which to find your needle!

The Very Real Relationship with Information Science

Information science used to be called "library science," a phrase that might conjure up memories of typed catalog cards in wooden drawers and the Dewey Decimal System. Metadata was also formerly called "cataloging." In the analog age, the cataloging of books, films, videos, and any media type was separate from the technology. The goal, however, was much the same as it is today: to describe materials in a way that would help users retrieve what they wanted.

University and public libraries use standard data structures and authorized forms of names and subjects to make searching for materials efficient. For broadcast and moving image materials, studios and networks were fortunate if they had a card or file system that tracked the date the material was shot or released; the program's title; a basic description; and the locations of the original elements, prints, videotapes, and associated materials.

Online catalogs and databases were quickly embraced by librarians and catalogers. While the focus of a catalog librarian's work remained the same (providing access to materials), catalog records in electronic form made searching far easier. They also eased the work involved in using standardized terms since global changes could be made by a few keystrokes instead of retyping cards or files. Keyword searching could be applied to titles, names, descriptions, and subject headings, in a way making data structures irrelevant.

Morphing from a manual cataloging and access environment to an electronic one required that library scientists work with the technology department for the first time. The library science staff became "clients" of the technology staff; they set the requirements for their data needs, which the technology department then implemented. As the world's business culture has passed from electronic to digital stages, where files are born or retrieved in digital format, the relationship between library science and technology has become (at least, it should have become) closer. Superficially, this has happened through nomenclature: "library science" has become "information science" to reflect how "librarians" now manage data creation and retrieval. "Cataloging" has become "metadata," to encompass not just the description of a physical object, but the creation of the digital file, its preservation, and all aspects of the essence the metadata describes. "Technology" has become "information technology" (or IT), charged with finding the means to track and retrieve metadata and digital files.

Businesses working with digital files, servers, and networks probably all have IT departments. However, not all businesses have a separate department in charge of the information science aspects of managing digital files. Perhaps since both concepts share the word "information," some might think that the IT department can perform both functions. But an IT staff is made up of engineers, application programmers, and database administrators, not necessarily trained in how to provide access to knowledge of content. Information science staff—those who know the content and know how current and future users, many unanticipated, will need to retrieve and manage it—are best qualified to create requirements for metadata creation and retrieval. In broadcasting, staff with information science roles can increasingly be found not just in the archive, but in several departments: program production, technical operations, the tape library, scheduling, and sales and licensing.

Data Structures, Rules, and Values

Inefficient data retrieval can occur when staff not trained in or aware of metadata business requirements and standards create data structures, rules, or values. *It is highly recommended that an organization try to use open standards whenever possible rather than reinvent the wheel.* Organizations and consortia of domain experts have already devoted years to creating these standards, so time can be saved by reviewing the available standards and adapting what is best for a particular environment. Besides saving staff time internally, using standards also benefits the organization when data must be shared externally—for example, in scheduling television programs for cable subscribers (TV-Anytime) or in licensing footage through a stock footage agency such as footage.net.

The concepts and some of the standards listed below will be discussed in more detail in Chapter 3.

Data Structure or Schema

The data structure is the overall record structure for all records in the database; it's the field list that is used. A schema describes the relationships between data elements. Examples of standardized data structures and schemas that can be used for television and broadcasting include the following:

SMPTE Descriptive Metadata, Scheme 1
SMPTE Metadata Dictionary, RP210
PB Core (Public Broadcasting)
International Federation of Television Archives (FIAT/IFTA) Minimum Data
Dublin Core
MPEG7
TV-Anytime
MARC21
Independent Media Arts Preservation (IMAP) Template (rather than a standard, the template is a software application that provides guidance to catalogers working in MARC or Dublin Core; it is mentioned here as an illustration of mapping between the two data structures).

Data Rules

While "data structures" define the fields that are used to create a record, "data rules" define the structuring of the data within a particular field. For example, should a person's name be written as Last-Name, First-Name, or as First-Name Last-Name (Doe, John or John Doe)? How should a title be written?

One might think that these rules don't matter in an age of keyword searching. However, if a researcher or producer needs a sorted list or report created off a particular field, inconsistent data will make for a frustrated client.

For example, let's say a producer wants a report on all the people interviewed on a particular program. She needs to see how many times individuals were interviewed over a span of five years. If a name were input without rules, it may appear as both Doe, Zevon and Zevon Doe, and the report could conceivably have entries for both forms of the name for the same person. The producer's aim could be frustrated, because she would not have accurate data if she did not look at the list past the letter "D."

There are many standards for data structures, but too few standards for data rules. The broadcasting community has not yet created any standardized data rules, but two have been created in the public sector:

- *Archival Moving Image Materials, version 2 (AMIM2).* These cataloging rules were created by the U.S. Library of Congress and were revised in 2000. The revised version contains enhanced sections for cataloging television and broadcasting materials and newsfilm (stock footage), and it has examples of records. AMIM is primarily used by the archival cataloging community (www.loc.gov/cds/catman.html#amima).
- *Anglo-American Cataloguing Rules, 2nd edition, 2002 revision (AACR2).* This manual has been in use by the English-speaking library science community since the 1960s. It does have a chapter on cataloging moving image materials, but since the creation of AMIM, most archival catalogers use AACR2 primarily for advice on formatting names. AACR2 is used as a descriptive standard primarily by public and academic libraries in cataloging commercial materials (e.g., DVDs for use in the library). While AACR2 is maintained by professional library science organizations in the United States, Canada, United Kingdom, and Australia, it is widely used as a standard in libraries around the world (www.aacr2.org/index.html).

Data Values

The actual content of a particular field or data element is the data value. In most cases, fields can contain text or numbers (in the case of date and item location fields), preferably following accepted data rules in formatting. For those fields used for indexing, it is best to use standard vocabularies, thesauri, or lists of authorized terms, names, subjects, and genres for the most efficient retrieval of materials. As with data rules, there are few standard data value lists of use in cataloging broadcasting programs. If standard lists are not used, an internal list of terms and names should be created to ensure consistent data input.

Some standardized data value lists in use in the United States are listed here. The European Community does not have many standard vocabularies, in part because of language differences across countries. The following standards will be discussed in more detail in Chapter 3.

- *IPTC: NewsCodes.* Includes both a subject list and a scene list (which defines production terms for scene types) (www.iptc.org/NewsCodes).

- *Moving Image Genre-Form Guide.* Compiled by staff at Library of Congress for common genre and form terms in film and broadcasting (www.loc.gov/rr/mopic/migintro.html).
- *Library of Congress Name Authority File (LCNAF).* The source for authorized forms of millions of personal and corporate names, titles, and other headings. This list is available on the Internet and can help keep forms of names consistent (http://authorities.loc.gov).
- *Library of Congress Subject Headings (LCSH).* These subject headings were designed to logically sort and display search results, as well as for retrieval. Consequently, headings can sometimes be long and unwieldy, but the basic forms of authorized headings can help keep terms consistent so users won't need to search both "purses" and "handbags" to find shots of handbags (http://authorities.loc.gov).

Metadata as the Key to Knowledge Management during the Production Processes

In a broadcasting production environment, incorrect or poorly created metadata can mean missed deadlines, not finding the right clip for the producer, and even mistakenly airing the wrong program because another show had a similar title but the metadata was not clear about which tape was which. Inaccurate data impacts all aspects of an end-to-end production environment, from the initial concept and planning stage, to distribution of clips on the Internet, to licensing footage years after production ends.

Metadata should be used to manage both information and knowledge about the production process and the content of a work and its manifestations (versions, copies, etc.). Those responsible for creating the metadata—and usually more than one person contributes to a metadata record—should create data with the user of 100 years in the future in mind. Unfortunately, in a fast-paced environment it is human nature to simply enter data in a shorthand that is meaningful to the person inputting the data but means nothing to the person sitting in the editing suite down the hall. This practice is especially deadly in a digital environment, where the only means to identify and retrieve files is through metadata.

Knowing What You've Got and Everything about It

Different users will need to know different things about the work, and the metadata record should be rich enough to serve any required current or envisaged future application (the richer the metadata, the more services can be served), though clearly in practice there may need to be some sort of prioritization. Production office staff might create the initial record (working title, key personnel, rights, etc.), with staff who work on the program through its production and air stages adding more information. The following list just scrapes the surface—it certainly is not intended to be anything other than thought-provoking. Perhaps it demonstrates how the majority of metadata is created "up front" in the production office and then lost, only for bits of it to be repeatedly recreated throughout the workflows of the production and archival lifecycles. Workflows are discussed in more detail in Chapter 2.

Program development and preproduction. Working title, genre, subjects, the program peg and structure, treatments and angles, conceptual and contextual information, key personnel, target air date, number of episodes, targeted slot, target audience, background research information on places and people (for example, do they sniff or mutter on air? Are they really an expert and just appear stupid? Is the chosen location dangerous? Does it rain a lot?), but above all—ideas.

Rights and licensing. Information on rights to use the material, both for external licensing footage and for the consumer to view on television on demand, over air (terrestrial or satellite), or over the Internet; rights for use of different components of the completed work such as the script, sound track, merchandising material, reuse, and retention.

Production. Financial information, location logistical information, lighting, location and shooting scripts, music details, personnel contact details (staffing, crewing, performers), contractual details, safety information or authorizations, technical details (high definition, widescreen, line standards, progressive or interlace, etc.), delivery information.

The shoot. Clapper board information, shot marking, contact details of any kind, tape numbers, take details, actuality details, key actions, shot listing, timecodes, cue words.

Archival research. Content information: subject, persons in a clip; date and location where footage was captured; unique identifier of tape or file.

Postproduction. Editor's notes, edit decision lists, rendering data, edited versions.

Scheduling. Traffic data, final title and description, running length, confirmed airdate.

Tape library. All information, including locations and unique identifiers for all copies of a work; any preservation information.

Web content developers. All information; locations of digital files to use for web clips.

Libraries as a Resource and Gold Mine

One compelling reason why a broadcaster should be concerned about maintaining accurate metadata is that it can contribute to an important revenue stream: repackaging series for the consumer video market, repurposing footage for internal use, and licensing footage to external buyers.

Film Studios

Over the past few decades, film studios have become well aware that the films in their libraries can be a revenue source long after the title's initial release. A film might be repackaged as "restored," a "special edition," or the "director's cut." These films may have long marketing lives on VHS cassette and (increasingly) DVD, with different releases or versions appearing even just a few months after the initial release. For example, the feature film *Lord of the Rings: Return of the King* had a normal theatrical run. Three months after the VHS/DVD versions appeared on the market, the "Special Extended Edition" (director's cut) was released.

Broadcast News

Broadcast news divisions have always understood the importance of maintaining at least a minimum amount of key metadata (subjects, people, locations, dates). Their own researchers and producers need to be able to quickly find clips to incorporate in their daily news programs and documentaries. This business requirement of tracking key shot metadata so footage can be found quickly benefited the broadcasters when they began selling outtakes from their libraries. The major broadcasters and stations often provide access to their stock footage databases through external agencies or licensing consortia. These agencies' websites sometimes provide digital previews of the footage so researchers can determine whether the footage contains what they need before they buy it. However, it is the accuracy of the metadata in the online database that brings the researcher to the footage and, it is hoped, to a sale for the broadcaster. Consistent and standardized metadata created by the broadcaster is key for researchers to find the footage they need.

Readers who have not yet initiated a metadata program might want to experiment searching across collections in the following licensing agencies' online databases to get a sense of why it is important to use standard field structures and vocabularies. When you create metadata, you have to think of not just how you and your company will use it, but also how external users will search for your footage (Figure 1.1).

- *www.FOOTAGE.net.* One-stop shopping for stock and archival footage. Participants include ABC News, CNN, Archive Films (Getty Images), HBO Sports Archive, NBC News, National Geographic Television Film Library, WGBH, WPA Film Library.
- *www.stockfootageonline.com.* BBC News and CBS News Archive footage for license.

Broadcast Entertainment

News divisions can license their footage. Broadcast entertainment divisions can sell videos (or DVDs) of their programs or series in the home video market, as well as television on demand (or TV-Anytime). Video sales of boxed sets of popular series include 1950s series such as *The Honeymooners* as well as more contemporary programs such as *The Sopranos* and *Sex and the City*.

Figure 1.1. CNN Library. Frame from raw footage of the fall of the Berlin Wall, November 10, 1989. For the metadata record, see the appendices.

The TV-Anytime Concept for the Use of Libraries

The TV-Anytime forum is a worldwide project involving vendors, broadcasters, telecommunications companies, and the consumer electronics industry, which has defined an extensive bundle of specifications for the use of local storage at home in a specialized "set-top box" or in the TV set. The forum aimed to identify all the potential possibilities enabled for the consumer by the use of home storage technology, to detail the consumer's requirements and aspirations for storing programs locally in the home and making them broadcast schedule independent, and to specify standard methodologies to implement the functionalities identified. All of the features heavily rely on metadata. In a later chapter, we will explore this in more detail.

A few of the business models from the TV-Anytime specification especially rely on the availability of content from libraries. A section of the business model specification says, "Once a program is selected via the ECG [Electronic Content Guide] an option shall be to record every episode of the program series." In the context of TV-Anytime, this means not only that all future episodes will be recorded but that the option exists to record all episodes that were transmitted in the past. To do this, a TV-Anytime based set-top box must be able to find this material from the library space, and therefore the metadata should be structured in such a way that the set-top box can find it automatically. The clear implication is that such metadata must be standardized so that basically every set-top in the world will be able to find the required content.

The mechanisms to achieve this are specified by the TV-Anytime forum. The content information needed by a TV-Anytime enabled set-top box should be made available by implementing service providers, and in many cases this information can be (automatically) extracted from a library file system. This information will have to be collected in advance, stored in the library's database, and made available to service providers in an unambiguous and uniform way.

Another TV-Anytime function is the ability to find and select related content. Related content can be "the making of" footage, "bloopers," or eventually the basic, raw material from the shoot. Metadata is essential to find this related content in order to link it to the completed program.

Where *Is* the Metadata?

This is a simple question and can be answered with a simple answer: everywhere. But this answer is deceptive and hides complex processes. In the digital world, there are two basic classes of metadata capture and storage: data embedded in the file (which currently is usually technical information about the file creation and playback) and metadata stored separately (usually descriptive and business data). These classes also have possible subclasses, offering a very detailed level of information.

Some technical metadata can be captured automatically and stored in the file itself. Often, such metadata tells machines the technical parameters they need to play the file. This class of metadata is very dark and obscure to nearly all users, especially when the file will not play at all and there is no clue as to why not. To read this technical metadata from the file, special software is needed. These kinds of tools are essential in determining the nature of a problem—for example, if the wrong player or decoder is being used or if the file is corrupted. However, fascinating though it is to technical folk, the subject of technical metadata is not a feature of this book and therefore will not be further mentioned in this context. For the purposes of this book, it is sufficient to say that technical metadata can be treated as part of the essence and is always embedded in the file header or stream.

Manually input metadata can appear in many forms and is usually stored separately from the digital file. In the analog video and audio world, there was no possibility of metadata storage in the analog signal (teletext or closed captioning is not metadata but data essence, although unknown (or "dark") metadata could be transported in the same space). Some basic information was stored on the tape or film container, and the description was on a card in a card file system or, a little more recently, in a computer database. The link between the two parts of the content was the program name and in many cases a number in the broadcaster's own numbering system. Program exchange between broadcasters and countries was not a very common activity, and the need for global exchange standards and uniqueness in identification was not pressing. The situation has changed rapidly with digital production and distribution and the demand for filling more and more hours of television and on-demand use. These applications and services have their own specific needs related to the availability of accurate metadata.

The two classes—data embedded in a file and data stored in a separate database—present questions like "How do we keep the metadata in the file synchronized with the metadata in the database all the time?" In making the decision on which kinds of data should be stored where, the data manager must consider several scenarios.

1. *Will the metadata be fixed/static or can it change or "grow"?* Usually people think of metadata as something static but in many cases it is not. Even legacy material must have updated metadata with the latest information to be effectively used in current projects. For example, when an actor or another person with an important role in the work dies, the date of death should be indicated in the metadata. For documentary program use, new facts about the footage need to be incorporated in the descriptive metadata. Rights metadata must be updated when there is a change in the rights situation or after the legal period has ended. Rights tracking can be very complex, especially when parts of the work have different rights holders and different rights are involved (e.g., music rights versus footage rights to use a small part of a framed picture). To implement these changes in the metadata efficiently, the best option is to have the metadata in a separate database and not embedded in the file. In cases where it is advisable to store and maintain complete metadata with the work (maybe for interchange, transport, or deep archiving), synchronization between the two parallel storage systems can be complex and costly.

   Note, though, that some metadata is dynamic and constantly changes with time rather than growing—some technical metadata falls into this category. Often, such metadata becomes useless with the passage of time and not worth storing.

2. *Is there a need for searching in the metadata?* Sometimes there is a need to search the metadata for keywords from a producer's, researcher's, or director's desktop computer. If this is achieved within an organization either via its local network or from outside the company, metadata embedded in the content file itself does not seem to be a practical solution. This is especially true if it is necessary to search from a remote location using the Internet without having available all the facilities of the corporate infrastructure. In this case, searching a separate metadata database will be a more practical solution, but it also will bring some restrictions in the searching process. When the metadata describes the content in a broad way it will not be a problem; but when the metadata is

addressing frame-related and tightly bound metadata, the search engine should display the metadata as it is coupled and related to that frame. In the future, more complex searching and playback facilities will become available. One day it will be possible to use a company's infrastructure to its full potential from any location in the world, but in the meantime we have to live with some restrictions and find practical ways of working around them. In the case of frame-bounded metadata, one needs at least to have real-time access to the content from a server that can handle this kind of searching over a network that is fast enough to perform this kind of action. It also puts extra demands on the metadata, as the extracted metadata should give information about the exact location in the file to which it applies. This suggests, besides the descriptive metadata, also a structured way of handling the time line information with the timed metadata. For this kind of application, storage in the file at the position where it is relevant seems a logical solution.

To handle this kind of metadata in synchronism with the essence, it is necessary to have the file online and accessible in a nonlinear fashion. This can be a costly solution, particularly when it applies to a large library at broadcast picture resolutions or even in visually lossless compressed formats, and it is likely to be very expensive at least for the near future.

A compromise alternative solution often can be found by storing material on a server as a low-resolution proxy version instead of the full broadcast resolution. However, the quality of this low-resolution proxy version needs to be good enough to enable making production decisions (such as identification or checking focus). In this way all kinds of hybrid combinations, from coupling metadata to the essence within the file or completely decoupling it from the essence and storing it in a separate database, may appear in practice.

3. *Is there a need for having the metadata available all the time?* One of the important questions is, "Is it necessary to have all metadata available online all the time?" Every advantage has its own balancing disadvantage. For example, an everything-on-demand-available-all-the-time type of system will have a high price tag. This will make a good return on investment difficult for archives and libraries. Therefore it is important to make a realistic calculation of the overall estimated operational costs of the metadata system.

Another important issue that all archives already face is the difficult question of what to archive out of all the produced material. It will be almost impossible to store all the raw material and the edited versions—not for technical reasons but due to sheer storage costs. In the digital realm, an organization must decide how its material will be stored: online, offline, or even "on the shelf." Other new questions will arise concerning the quality of the material available, access speed, and completeness (essence plus metadata), among others.

4. *Will the content be used for further processing, and what will happen with the metadata?* In the case where the content is on a server or data tape with the meta-

data bounded to individual frames—for example, interaction TV data used for production or transmission—a few other interesting questions and problems will arise.

This will be the case especially if the material with embedded metadata needs to be switched or keyed with some other content stream, which also may be a file with embedded metadata. The metadata embedded in the file cannot easily be handled by switching or mixing equipment—partly because current equipment cannot handle it and partly because decisions about what to do with the metadata are necessary—and therefore it will need to be stripped out of the content and parallel processed in a metadata "mixer." After the mix, the correct metadata should be determined and embedded in the resulting content. The success of this process depends on the application used and its implementation, because many variables can creep in.

For example, whenever two streams (A and B, say) are mixed or added together in some way, the resulting content may or may not have the original A or the original B metadata because what happens during the mix depends on the application. The output metadata may be replaced with new metadata after the mix. Or the resulting metadata may depend on values of variables in the A or the B metadata or any combination of these. The relative timing of the output metadata might also be important (Figure 1.2), and synchronization can often be a major headache!

The database where the stripped-off metadata is going during the mix process must be a complex machine with a lot of onboard intelligence, and the metadata switch functions should be coupled with the functions in the mixing device. After mixing, the metadata should have the correct timing relationships, eventually in synchronism with the relevant audio and video.

What happens during the duration of the transition depends on the situation and the specific needs of the program. This can lead to a complex data management situation, and in the near future such mixing or cutting will have to be carried out

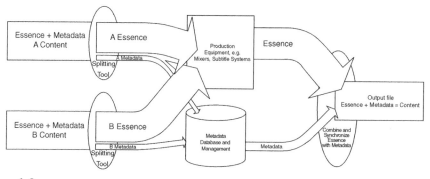

Figure 1.2.

between two programs with associated interaction or statistics metadata and the decisions made will be much more important and far reaching than at present.

Will the metadata "mixer" in the diagram be similar in operation to a mixer used in the current audio and video streams? Most likely not. The metadata mixer is likely to be an IT device or subsystem managed in a way that permits only the correct metadata to associate with the right spot in the audio or video signal. IT engineers in this area will need skills in broadcast technology as well as in IT to manage and implement this kind of infrastructure.

Metadata Synchronization

In the preceding examples, we mentioned synchronized metadata several times. Until late in 2004, this kind of metadata rarely existed in currently produced content. In most cases, descriptive metadata is a description of the content as a whole. Sometimes there will be some information about individual shots or scenes in the form of a time-code list with information at the listed time-codes. In other words, time line information is linked to the metadata.

With a new generation of television programs on the horizon that allows people to react to or interact with specific elements in the content at specific times, it will be necessary to have information available at the specific frames, shots, or scenes. This is synchronizing metadata, available on a time line, coupled with the essence and most likely in one container or wrapper. Recently developed file exchange standards define mechanisms to achieve this effect—that is, to link with the time line. Metadata becomes time accurate because it is on the same time line as the essence.

These recent file exchange standards allow for more video, audio, and metadata streams. For example, there can be parallel metadata tracks in different languages or more than one form of interaction metadata track so that users can interactively work with the content in a way that is specific to an area or culture. Such possibilities in the transport or exchange formats of programs allow for interesting new program concepts developed with a high level of automation to help control costs.

One important issue to take into account will be the difference in process time in the different delivery channels to the consumer—there are big variations across the diversity of delivery channels. The whole issue of synchronizing metadata becomes ever more complicated as content is delivered using more delivery methods, each with its own properties and characteristics. For instance, each channel of audio, video, and metadata will inevitably have its own processing and transmission delay between the transmitter and the consumer. Mixing this content will be difficult—particularly if the channels are routed separately, with the video delivered by satellite, say, and the metadata delivered via the Internet. The results of this process for audio and video are already evident in today's transmissions, and the implications for metadata are often not yet even considered.

2 Types of Metadata

Metadata is used in different ways by those people involved in making and publishing television programs and those people who consume them. These two communities sit on either side of an imaginary boundary of publication—whether that publication is transmitted through traditional terrestrial broadcasting, via satellite, over the Internet, or by a DVD sent through the regular mail. Yet much of the metadata used by both communities is the same—titles, genre, slot, business information such as rights, and so on.

Later in this chapter, we will look at the workflow of program production and the metadata associated with each stage. Before that, however, it is worthwhile to consider metadata under three main headings: Descriptive, Business/Legal (sometimes called Administrative), and Preservation, each broadly related to *purpose* rather than *workflow*.

The "Purpose" of Metadata

Descriptive

As its name implies, *descriptive* metadata provides a description of program content, often including access points (name, subject, and genre/form headings, etc.). It can include three main areas in the metadata record: a narrative summary of the program (brief and/or long versions), a list of the subjects explored in the program, and a suggestion about the genre of the show. "Subject" is what the program is about, regardless of whether it is a nonfiction or fictional program. "Genre" is what the program is: comedy, drama, sports, news, Western, and so on.

Several people can add descriptive metadata as the program evolves through the idea to playout stages. The key issue is for contributors to be consistent in how the metadata is added (terms used and rules followed) so that everyone involved provides information useful to the production team, company, archive, and consumer, with minimal duplication of effort. Some descriptive metadata can be used for program guides, as well as in the marketing and consumer areas. The cataloger or library science professional in charge of maintaining the metadata database should consult with these other business units to ensure that useful and easily understood terms are applied unambiguously across the enterprise. Descriptive metadata can be added as early as the initial idea stage, along with a working or even final title (which is *identification* metadata). For example, the producer could add terms for the subject and genre of the program, since the topic of the show was most likely decided from the beginning.

Subject metadata includes terms that describe the topic(s) of the show. Often, this metadata appears in a general keyword field. However, it could help the catalogers (and staff needing to find a particular program) if the catchall keyword field were broken out into discrete subject-related fields. Types of subject metadata can include the following:

- Names (in the case of a show profiling a person or a company)
- Geographic places (both the actual location where a scene was shot—for example, Burbank, California—and the virtual location it was meant to depict—such as the Sinai Desert)
- Historical events or periods (World War II, Berlin Wall, etc.)
- Topical nouns (football, fashion, global warming, etc.)

Ideally, the cataloger should select names and terms from a controlled vocabulary or thesaurus so that indexing, search, and retrieval are more accurate. Even if the cataloger does not utilize lists of open source vocabularies, an internal standardized list should still be created and followed. The concept of controlled vocabularies is discussed in more detail in Chapter 3.

Genre terms would ideally be added at the beginning of the program's life cycle. Genre describes the type of program, such as news, children's programming, or drama. Usually there will be one genre term, but at times there can be more than one. For example, a children's program might also be classified as a news broadcast (for example, Nickelodeon's *Nick News*).

Narrative *summaries* often come in two varieties: long and short. The short summary is usually one sentence and is often used in programming guides. The longer narrative (up to a paragraph or two) is usually for internal use, but it is sometimes also provided on the program's website for fuller episode descriptions and enriched keyword searching. The long narratives are generally written after the program has been completed and is ready to broadcast. Short summaries can be written at any time in the production process.

Administrative

Administrative metadata includes *business* and *legal* metadata and can be attached to a program produced by the company or to programs licensed by the broadcaster. At a minimum, business and legal metadata should track information surrounding the creation of the program (names of persons involved in production, contracts with talent, licenses to shoot at a particular location, etc.), who owns the intellectual property rights to the program, and any information on the program's use and permissions.

In the digital environment, legal metadata is often linked to *digital rights management (DRM)*. Several levels of information about a program need to be tracked for the legal department, from licensing and contracts relevant to the production of the program to on-demand restrictions and permissions for the consumer. Legal metadata usually contains date-sensitive information, since contracts and rights can expire.

For production, the metadata record can make reference to contracts with talent and production staff, licenses for locations, and other particulars that are held on file in the legal department. Not all the legal information needs to be retained with every instantiation of the program.

As mentioned later in this chapter, the archive might not care about the access license with the owner of a field where a scene was shot. That information need not be embedded in a digital file of the program. However, the contract or license information does need to be retained in the legal department's files. *All* legal and business metadata should be archived, even though it might be relevant to only a few specialized departments. Those who do not need the information may be prevented from viewing it by limiting their access for reasons of confidentiality. Not many people would like their personal or financial details freely available throughout an organization.

Public archives that hold television and broadcasting materials should track, at a minimum, who owns the *rights* to the programs, or parts of programs, and any usage restrictions. It is worth pointing out that this metadata is *dynamic* and can (and frequently will) change with the passage of time. Provenance information (e.g., how the archive acquired the materials) should also be permanently retained.

Preservation

Production entities have a strong business interest in preserving their assets so the programs or their component parts can be reused in the future (footage repurposed, extended cuts released, programs released on video, etc.). Public archives that perform preservation activities for the programs in their care also need to track this information and sometimes even share it with fellow archives so that the preservation effort is not duplicated.

Preservation metadata tracks the *condition* of the physical or digital forms of the program and any actions taken to preserve them. For analog materials, this can include noting when a tape was transferred to another medium or new film elements struck. For digital materials, preservation activities can include tracking when a digital file is backed up or transferred to another storage medium. Information that should be tracked includes the following:

- The action taken (file backed up, tape transferred, etc.)
- Where the action took place (at the studio, lab, etc.)
- The date the action took place
- Any condition concerns (original tape has sticky shed, the digital file is corrupt, etc.)

Metadata in the Workflow

The Metadata of Program Production and Publication

Chapter 1 referred to one person's important metadata being another person's rubbish. This is a key difficulty as we move into the new digital age and begin to implement the new workflows enabled by this new technology.

For example, at the program planning stage when a reconnaissance for a location shoot is being carried out, little thought is probably being given to the needs of the archivist at the end of the program-making chain—even though location details that might be useful in the future will certainly be known. Conversely, the archivist will probably see little need for knowing who owned the field where the shoot took place or what the access arrangements were. Neither of them would be particularly interested in playout automation metadata—though advertising clients most certainly would be!

Each part of the planning workflow makes its own contribution to the finished program—right from the morning shower (where all the best ideas are born) through researching, commissioning, production, postproduction, indexing and cataloging in the library, and on to publication (playout). However, the point in the process where a piece of metadata first becomes available is not necessarily a point where it is needed for that stage in the process. Worse, frequently two or more stages in the workflow might need the same metadata, but not the intervening processes. For example, the camera operator on a news shoot will certainly know the tape cassette numbers, and the picture editor will certainly need to know them. But the newsroom journalists who scripted the story might not need the cassette numbers because journalists sometimes do not need to look at the tapes, even though the dispatch rider brings them all back to the newsroom. So the picture editor gets lots of scripted stories and lots of tapes—but which belongs to which?

Each workflow stage will have it own specialist metadata. Some metadata will be common to many or nearly all stages. Clearly, it makes sense to capture metadata

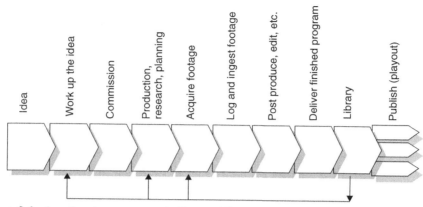

Figure 2.1. A notional program production workflow.

at the earliest stage possible as a program is made, and to either pass it through the chain or hold it in a common repository. This way, those stages that need the metadata can access it easily and do not need to look for it, reacquire it, or, worse, reinvent it. Sadly, this has *not* been the traditional way of doing things.

The notional workflow illustrated in Figure 2.1 is not real, but is intended as an example of the process stages commonly encountered in a program production workflow. The emphasis placed on each stage will depend on the nature of the program. For example, the planning process required for a news program is very different from that necessary for a period drama. In both cases planning is essential; only the scale and depth changes. Likewise, the commissioning process is different; but here again, someone has to give the go-ahead and make the resources available. The breakouts which follow give some idea of the information being created and used at each stage.

All programs derive from someone's original idea. Sometimes the idea is forced upon an organization (as is the case with many news stories); other times the idea originates from a sponsoring or commissioning body, from a member of the public, or from a work in another medium (for example, from a book). Frequently though, the idea comes in a flash of inspiration that might take form when the

Figure 2.1a. person is taking a shower, commuting to work, or even eating dinner.

Unremarkably, even at the outset the idea will bring with it some metadata: what the program will be about (the subject), its genre, the likely target audience, and maybe the best date or time to show the program. A short summary of the program idea will be jotted down, to be used later. Quickly following on from this will be thoughts about the best medium (film or TV), possible actors and artists for the lead roles, key contributors, and whether the program will be a single blockbuster or a series of episodes. There will already be some sketchy outline of the business implications—who would be best to make the program, the research involved, and likely implications for intellectual property and rights.

Most of this will be jotted down for later consideration—nearly always on paper, sometimes in a word-processing document. Rarely is the idea widely shared at this stage—good ideas are very valuable intellectual property and are therefore jealously guarded.

Work up the idea

Having slept on the idea and decided to run with it, facts of life dictate that funding becomes an immediate issue. Someone needs to be persuaded to pay for making the program. Few ideas are sufficiently brilliant to let this happen immediately and in isolation, so in practice "samples" have to be "sold" to a likely financier, alongside the idea itself, to demonstrate the feasibility, quality, and sheer brilliance of the program concepts. The summary of the program that was jotted down at the idea stage will be worked up to advertise or sell the idea. Program making is still expensive, so the costs are likely to be considerable and the time with a potential backer will be short. The sales pitch has to be good, persuasive, and able to withstand searching questions about all aspects of the project.

Figure 2.1b.

Seed resources will have to be allocated to work up the idea and shape it into a "proper" project. Allocating resources and the setting up of a project straight away implies documented project information and hence more metadata: the project will have to be allocated some sort of project number, it will acquire a working name or title, cost control and budgeting information become a priority, and staff have to be allocated to tasks. Research needs to be carried out into feasibility by finding answers to a series of pertinent questions, such as: Have similar ideas already been realized? Is there existing art in the library that can be used as a resource for contacts or background material? Does usable and maybe previously unused footage already exist, and, if so, is it accessible at a reasonable cost? Is the program concept sound and does it stand up to scrutiny, or does it need to be changed? What is the best way to treat the idea? Are the best performers available in the right timescale and at the right cost? Does music need to be written especially for the program or can existing recordings be used? Where is the best place to make the program—on location, in a studio, or a mixture of the two? Is the best location affordable? Who will produce and edit the demonstration samples?

Commission

Once the idea has been sold, things begin to get serious. Moves are made in many directions at once, and whoever decides to finance the development of the idea into a proper production by commissioning it will have his or her own views.

First, and perhaps most important of all, business details need to be thrashed out, such as the exact terms and conditions, prices, costs, payment details and terms, and bank particulars. Rights become an

Figure 2.1c.

issue now. Which rights are to be retained and which sold? Are there any rights implications for the input material and resources? Will the idea or format be licensed to only one organization or sold to many organizations internationally? Timescales and delivery details need to be agreed upon, along with stage payments and authorization or approval authorities.

The commissioner will want his or her own stamp on the look and treatment of the program and how it is structured and will have ideas for the distribution media and how publication will be scheduled. Commissioners may have conditions too on the choice of artists for key roles, such as who directs or edits the program and who composes the music, and they may even want to peg the scheduling to an upcoming or past event.

Now the technical metadata starts to rear its head as part of the delivery detail. How will the program be delivered? On tape in traditional cassette format? As a computer file to be played out from a server (and if so, to what standard)? What will be the aspect ratio? Standard definition—525 NTSC or 625 PAL? High definition—720 or 1080 lines? Progressive or interlace scanning? What compression scheme should be used? Is stereo or surround sound the best choice, and what scheme is preferred?

On top of that, what are the commissioner's requirements for metadata? Are there interactive metadata requirements? Does the delivered program need to come with a simple abstract or fully indexed and cataloged—and if so, to what standard?

Production, research, planning

Figure 2.1d.

This is the major stage in the making of a program. In spite of what people involved in postproduction work or in technical departments would have you believe, this is where the program is actually pulled together and made ready for assembling. This is also where the bulk of program-related metadata is produced. The work done during the working-up stage earlier will be revisited and now forms the basis for serious development work in combination with any requirements that the commissioner has made.

Resourcing has to be properly worked out and budgeted, which includes everything from casting the onscreen personalities (and their terms for taking part) to the availability, costs, and other details for useful experts, experienced researchers, and camera and postproduction personnel. Locations have to be found and reconnoitered, possibly meaning that hotels, transportation, catering, and toilet facilities might have to be arranged. Rights to existing material must be negotiated and any safety or policing issues identified and resolved. None of this can be left to chance, and a huge amount of legwork is involved in the necessary research.

Initial contracts have to be placed to "lock in" the agreed arrangements, and the resulting business issues need to be tracked and documented. There will be endless discussions in the production offices about all the aspects and details of the program as it comes to together—not to mention the frustrations as things do not go according to plan (even these are worth noting for later reference). Seemingly endless background research has to be carried out.

Then, at last, scripts can be pulled together—not only traditional participants' scripts for speech, but also scripts for cameras, lighting, sound, and so on.

Acquire footage

Probably 80 percent of the work has been done now, and shooting new footage (material) for the program or acquiring suitable existing material can begin.

This can be an iterative process, and the material will grow throughout the production process from now on, seemingly of its own accord. From this stage of the process on, it pays off to log and store as much of the metadata as possible as it becomes available during the production process: descriptions of scenes, shots, light conditions, camera positions, participants, times, costumes, and anything else that can be recorded. Documenting this information will pay off handsomely at the end of production. Sometimes metadata becomes available which is not used until later—the temptation is to not capture it now to save time, but this is a very false economy.

Figure 2.1e.

Increasingly, devices that capture pictures or sound can automatically record much of the technical metadata from their own control systems—cameras that keep track of f-stop, filter wheel settings, and focal length are obvious examples. Likewise, it is becoming common for devices to capture the time of day and date and even the latitude, longitude, and altitude of their position when recording of the clip started. Perhaps most important of all, many modern devices generate and record a globally unique identifier for the particular clip of material at the very instant the record button is pressed and have facilities to import metadata from the production office database and combine it into the output.

Log and ingest footage

If the metadata logging has taken place during shooting, this task will be much simpler and more accurate than for material that is logged sometime later or when legacy material is logged. It has traditionally been common practice for the logging to be started in earnest only when the recordings have been returned to the production center— frequently a researcher or production assistant would sit down and view the tapes and log them at the same time. With analog recordings from the camera, logging this information is not inconvenient because it can be combined with the tedious task of ingesting the material into a digital system. However, as more cameras and audio recorders capture material directly into the digital domain, the former method will become an increasingly inefficient way of working.

Figure 2.1f.

All information necessary to produce or to find segments of material must be properly structured and documented at this stage, and missing information should be added to the project whenever this is possible. Finding or re-creating it later is at best inefficient and at worst prone to error. Examples in the case of a documentary program would be logging scene changes or producing an "as recorded" transcript of an interview for use when searching the archive or when a book is to be produced as a supplement to the program. Increasingly, scene change detection and speech recognition software will be used at this stage. So, too, will tools to describe the content in analytical terms of the image itself—color, texture, scene depth, and so on—as these details will become easier to capture and stored metadata will be able to include them, possibly as histograms, for use later. This development will enable searching using techniques that are less crude than the current method of using text-based descriptions—for example, in searching by shape, texture, or timbre, or by image matching and even face or voice recognition.

Post produce, edit, etc.

In the recent past, at this work stage the only metadata stored with the content was the edit decision list (EDL). This list contained, at a minimum, the duration of the shot and the information about the switch between one scene and the other (the "in-point" and the "out-point"). The list represented the switching or rendering that must be applied to the original recorded material to produce the final output; traditionally, this is done offline and not always in real time, but increasingly it can be done in real time as high-speed processing makes it feasible.

Figure 2.1g.

At its simplest, the EDL has only the switch points in terms of time-codes. Nowadays, more complex operations call for information about transitions, image manipulation, and rendering, and a lot more information needs to be stored, particularly if the material needs further postproduction at, for example, another facility or if it will be reused or repurposed. Machine settings, digital effect settings, and audio mixing information all need to be stored with the original recorded material if it ever needs to be seamlessly used again in the way it was used before, as would happen, for example, with producing different versions or alternative cuts.

Deliver finished program

Until recently, programs have been delivered in a straightforward way—usually in a can, transported in a van or on a trolley to wherever they were needed for playout or storage. A simple adhesive label served as sufficient identification, and if the program was in several parts, the appropriate cans were simply taped together.

The introduction of new digital technologies changes this fundamentally. Not only can a finished program be delivered electronically, but the deliverables can be expected to change and be more comprehensive—for example, an interactive program will not only have the main video and audio material, but it will also contain the metadata and supplementary material necessary for the program to

Figure 2.1h.

interact correctly with the end consumer. In future contracts, the required descriptive, cataloging, administrative, and other metadata may well be stipulated in the commissioning contract as part of the delivery schedule. Electronic delivery also implies greater reliance on the business system, with its need for accurate metadata and unambiguous identification.

Figure 2.1i.

The *library* can nowadays be considered the repository where actively used tapes, files, and metadata are stored. Metadata associated strictly with library functions need not be as detailed or extensive as that for the associated archive, as is often reflected by the function being distributed under a number of names given to the library such as "current operations library," "playout store," "transmission shelf," or simply "incoming."

The benefit of the library is that it can quickly retrieve a program for a producer to view or use the footage, or for broadcast operations to air the show. Metadata required for library purposes can vary depending on the particular circumstances and application and can include identification facts (title, episode title or number, program number, tape location), technical and playout information (running time, tape or digital file format), descriptive metadata (subject, genre, summary), abbreviated production information (director, producer, cast), and initial airdate. A prime function of the library is that it is a readily available source of material for any purpose: an authoritative source of facts and figures, research for another program, stock footage, repurposed usage of existing material (either unseen or previously used), and even ideas and treatments.

Somewhat in contrast, the *archive* has come to be the repository where more extensive metadata is stored in perpetuity along with any related material, both essences and other information. Information on physical items, such as condition and preservation information, is also kept in the metadata. For items kept as digital files, the error rates and other technical parameters for recent accesses will be logged for automatic system alert purposes. Archival metadata will contain all the information the library holds, but added to it will be legal, administrative, preservation, audience statistics, and other metadata that provides the fuller picture of the program's creation and history.

All metadata contributors should keep a basic archival principle in mind: metadata is added not for you or your immediate needs but for users 100 years or more from now. This principle is difficult to implement in a fast-paced production environment, but it should be the goal. It stresses the importance of consistent metadata and clear but concise contributions. A user 100 years from now should be able to read a metadata record and understand the program's production intentions, contents, and whole life cycle as well as its audience and how the physical manifestations were created.

At some point the program will be ready for consumption and must be prepared for distribution. For a traditional broadcast, the correct file must be identified,

scheduled, and made available to the playout system. For a digital broadcast, additional service information (SI) must be made available, and in the case of interactive television the application must be made available as well. All the components that together form the interactive TV program should be multiplexed into the digital broadcast stream. Interactive digital broadcast services rely heavily on metadata and its correctly timed injection into the broadcast program.

In reality, many more playout combinations and possibilities exist. Digital terrestrial, cable, satellite, and the Internet all have their own specific needs, usually controlled by the metadata that comes with

Figure 2.1j.

the file. Currently the information needed can be (and frequently is) produced and assembled at this stage, but it is likely that in the future it will be collected during the stage of production at which it first becomes available.

Metadata Flow

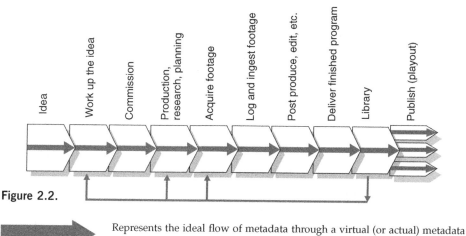

Figure 2.2.

Represents the ideal flow of metadata through a virtual (or actual) metadata repository, which is continuous throughout the workflow.

Figure 2.2 gives an impression of a complete production chain where a metadata repository has been positioned as a central connection between the different workflow stages.

In practice, this repository would be the central metadata database of a production organization. The figure can be redrawn to demonstrate an overarching metadata repository and to show how metadata is not used at every stage in the workflow, with each workflow stage requesting the metadata it needs, updating

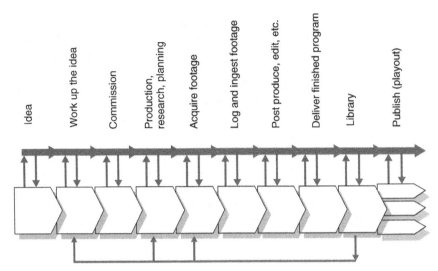

Figure 2.3.

that metadata, and passing it back or adding the data created in this stage into the repository rather than having all the workflow metadata passing though every stage whether it was used or not.

By the time the program is finalized, the metadata should be as complete as possible and ready for transmission, retransmission, or exchange by other means. At a minimum, it must contain all the components needed to configure the different (possibly interactive) playout channels and the metadata modules that should be transmitted with the program.

The central metadata database can be provided with templates for each stage in the production process and/or for each individual in the process, to restrict or filter the metadata elements so that each user has access to only those elements needed for that particular process. As can be appreciated from the brief outlines of the workflow presented earlier, the metadata can be roughly categorized under distinct headings: metadata purely descriptive of the program content, metadata for business and administration, metadata for archival use (indexing, cataloging, etc.), and so on.

The Metadata of Program Publication and Consumption

Chapter 3 will describe some of the existing metadata standards for broadcasting. Regardless of the actual metadata standard used, metadata records for television production, distribution, and consumers should contain most of the following elements, which are based on the metadata elements found in the Society of Motion Picture and Television Engineers' (SMPTE's) Recommended Practice RP210 and Descriptive Metadata Scheme 1 Standard, SMPTE380M. Many of these elements appear obvious, but they still must be specified if interoperability is to be achieved. Note that these elements are not taken from any real application. The following table is only an example and does include some technical descriptive metadata elements that might be included in the archive record.

Titles	Titling metadata relating to productions
Title kind	Kind of title (i.e., project, group of programs, group of series, series, item, program, working, original, item, episode, element, scene, shot, etc.)
Main title	The main title
Secondary title	The secondary title
Series number	The alphanumeric series number
Episode number	The alphanumeric episode number
Scene number	The alphanumeric scene number
Take number	Take number of the instance of the shot
Version title	The version title
Mission identifier	A locally defined identifier for the platform mission number
Working title	The (possibly temporary) working title of a production or a production component
Original title	The original title of a production
Clip number	The alphanumeric number of the clip
Brand main title	Main brand title (e.g., Horizon)
Brand original title	Any original brand title
Framework title	A human readable title for this instance of the production framework (e.g., "Wilco Productions version 3")
Product	Abstract information about the media product
Kind of programming group	The kind of program group of which the program forms a part (e.g., anthology, serial, series, themed cluster, repeating series)
Title of programming group	The title of a programming group
Total number of episodic items	Total number of episodic items in a series

Total number of series in a series group	The total number of series for a related group of series (For example, several series of the same program may be commissioned over many years.)
Episode item start number	The episodic number at the start of a series
Rights	Rights metadata
Copyright	Copyright metadata
Copyright status	Executive evaluation of copyright status
Copyright owner	The name of the person/organization who owns the copyright
Permitted access	Details of permitted access to the media product
Restrictions on use	Identifies the type or level of restriction applied to the media product
Security	Content encryption/decryption information
Broadcast	Broadcast outlet information
Broadcaster	The broadcasting organization
Name	Name of the broadcasting organization
Channel	Broadcast channel
Service	The broadcast service (e.g., News 24)
Publishing medium	Publishing medium, including transmission (e.g., satellite, cable, terrestrial)
Publishing medium code	Code defining the publishing medium, including transmission (e.g., satellite, cable, terrestrial)
Broadcast region	Target region of broadcast
General publication	General publishing details
Name	Name of the publishing organization
Publication service	The publication service
Publishing medium	Publishing medium, including transmission (e.g., satellite, cable, terrestrial)
Publication region	Target region of publication
Broadcast and repeat information	Business information concerning the production
Broadcast flags	Flags concerning aspects of business or administration

First broadcast flag	First broadcast of the product
Repeat numbers	Information about the repeat status when not a first broadcast
Current repeat number	The number of the current repeat
Previous repeat number	The number of the previous repeat
Event start true date—time (date, hours, minutes, seconds, fractions of seconds)	The absolute beginning date and time of the project, mission, scene, editing event, license, publication, etc.
Event start date and time— UTC	The absolute beginning date and time of the project, mission, scene, editing event, license, publication, etc.
Event start date and time— local time (default = undefined)	The absolute beginning date and time of the project, mission, scene, editing event, license, publication, etc.
Event end true date—time (date, hours, minutes, seconds, fractions of seconds)	The absolute ending date and time of the project, mission, scene, editing event, license, publication, etc.
Event end date and time— UTC	The absolute ending date and time of the project, mission, scene, editing event, license, publication, etc.
Event end date and time— local time (default = undefined)	The absolute ending date and time of the project, mission, scene, editing event, license, publication, etc.
Ratings	Information about audience ratings and indices
Audience rating	Audience rating as number of viewers
Audience reach	The audience reach of the production
Audience share	The audience share expressed as a percentage
Audience appreciation	The appreciation index of the program, expressed as points out of 100
Language codes for spoken language	Language codes that represent the language used for speech
Primary language	ISO 639 Language Code for the current primary spoken language
Secondary language	ISO 639 Language Code for the current secondary spoken language
Original primary language	ISO 639 Language Code for the original primary spoken language

Original secondary language	ISO 639 Language Code for the original secondary spoken language
Primary extended language code	ISO 639 Extended Language Code for the current primary spoken language with optional country variant
Secondary extended language code	ISO 639 Extended Language Code for the current secondary spoken language with optional country variant
Original extended primary language	ISO 639 Extended Language Code for the original primary spoken language with optional country variant
Original extended secondary language	ISO 639 Extended Language Code for the original secondary spoken language with optional country variant
Language names	Language names
Language name	The International Standards Organization name for a language
Content classification	Content classification
Content coding system	The system of coding for program classification (e.g., Escort 2.4)
Program type	Type of program (e.g., cartoon, film)
Genre	Program genre (e.g., entertainment, current affairs magazine, Italo Western)
Target audience	Target audience (e.g., children, 17 to 32, elderly)
Program material classification code	The resulting delineated classification code from the classification system
Textual description	A textual characterization of the data set
Abstract	A brief narrative summary of the data set
Purpose	A summary of the intentions with which the data set was developed
Description	A freeform textual description
Color descriptor	For example, black and white or tinted
Format descriptor	For example, Letterbox or Pillarbox
Intent descriptor	A freeform textual description written before production implementation and so on started (e.g., at the scripting stage)

Textual description kind	A summary of the use for which the description was made (e.g., billings, the production company's original description, a full production description)
Group synopsis	Synopsis of the group, series, serial, etc.
Annotation synopsis	Synopsis of the A/V content
Annotation description	A free-form textual description of the A/V content
Scripting kind	Description of the scripting kind as a text string (e.g., lighting, transcript, etc.)
Scripting text	The scripting text string
Shot description	A freeform textual description of the shot defined by this set
Annotation kind	The kind of annotation (e.g., technical, editorial, archival)
Related material description	A freeform textual description of related material of any kind
Awards	Awards relating to editorial, technical, or other aspects of the content and contributors to it
Individual	Awards granted to individuals
Program	Awards granted to program
Festival	The festival or award ceremony at which an award was made
Award name	Name of the award
Award classification	Name of the award classification
Nomination category	Nomination category of the award (e.g., best actor, best director)
Qualitative values	Assessed values relating to editorial, technical, and other aspects of the content and contributors to it
Asset values	Assessment of the program quality
Content value	Assessment of the content value
Cultural quality	Assessment of the cultural quality
Aesthetic value	Assessment of the aesthetic quality
Historic value	Assessment of the historic value

Technical value	Assessment of the technical value
Other values	Assessment of other relevant qualities
Aspect ratios	The horizontal-to-vertical aspect ratio of the image
Presentation aspect ratio	The horizontal-to-vertical aspect ratio of the whole image as it is to be presented to avoid geometric distortion and hence including any black edges
Capture aspect ratio	The horizontal-to-vertical aspect ratio of the image captured at the sensor—hence after the (possibly anamorphic) lens
Viewport aspect ratio	The horizontal to vertical aspect ratio of the image viewport (i.e., the desired shot as it is framed for capture and thus the aspect ratio at which the image must be viewed to avoid geometric distortion)
Digital video/image signal type identifiers	Identifiers of the specific standard to which a video signal conforms
Digital video/image compression parameters	Information about the digital video compression scheme used (MPEG, DV, etc.)
Digital audio processing parameters	Parameters required for processing
Video/image compression	Information about video or image compression
Audio compression	Information about audio compression
Audio compression algorithm	Algorithms used, bitrates used, modes used
Data essence compression	Information about data essence compression
Metadata compression	Information about metadata compression
Noise reduction processing	Information about any noise reduction process
Video noise reduction process	Information about any video noise reduction
Audio noise reduction process	Information about any audio noise reduction
Audio noise reduction algorithm	Algorithm used in a noise reduction process (e.g., Dolby SR, Telcom)

3 Metadata Schemes, Structures, and Encoding

First, it is important not to confuse metadata structures and schemes with how they are encoded for use within a digital system. This is easy to do and is one of the most common causes of misunderstanding. It is important to be clear that what a metadata element *is* (a list of elements in a metadata structure or dictionary) and how it is *used* (metadata scheme) has nothing whatsoever to do with how it is *encoded* for that use. Example encoding schemes are key-length-value (KLV), used for wrapping video or audio data into computer files between media servers, and eXtensible Mark-up Language (XML), frequently used for wrapping metadata into computer files between databases in the form of XML schema.

Metadata Schemes and Structures

Earlier, we touched on the differences between data, information, and knowledge. We have also looked at some of the sorts of metadata to be found during the program-making workflow and identified some of the metadata items (or elements) that might be found at each stage.

To convey information, however, these metadata elements have to be combined into groupings. This is so that component parts that belong together are kept together, in very much the same way as, in natural language, words are grouped together to form meaningful sentences—for example, when an adjective is safely tied to the word that it describes or modifies. If the rules of grammar are not followed in a natural language, the result can be at best confusing and at worst unintelligible, though usually a human being can sort things out (for example, the phrases "a koala eats, shoots and leaves," or "the piano was bought by the lady with the carved legs"). The same applies to metadata—if the rules for grouping and structuring metadata are not followed, little or no useful information will be conveyed. Worse, what is conveyed might appear okay but in fact be erroneous.

Clearly, metadata schemes are likely to be complex structures although built up from simple metadata elements: metadata elements arranged in groups, the groups in turn arranged into larger groups or groups of groups (these are sometimes called frameworks), and so on to form a scheme. In essence, a model is built up of the metadata in such a way as to preserve contextual and semantic relationships. Data modeling is a well-evolved and complex discipline. Numerous books have been written on the subject, and several modeling languages are in current use. Many good introductory books on the subject are also available, so we will not explore it further here.

In practice, it has been customary in many parts of the program-making workflow to be sloppy about applying metadata rules. Generally, this has caused few problems because the human mind can look at the metadata and quite quickly work out what the original intent was or apply the rules retrospectively, particularly in the case of someone familiar with that stage in the workflow. But with machines handling the metadata, the story is different—they are easily confused and apply no intelligence.

Confusingly, too, the different communities involved with program making have often intended different meanings by the same words—archivists, broadcast engineers, and information technology folk frequently have differing understandings of words such as "groups," "structure," "encoding," or "schemes." Even terms like "collection," "dataset," and "type" have completely different meanings to different communities. This is understandable in view of the diverse directions from which the communities come—library science, electronics, and data handling. However, the assorted interpretations frequently lead to misunderstanding and can result in a lack of trust between the disciplines. This inconsistency even applies at the top level of systemization. For instance, the Society of Motion Picture and Television Engineers (SMPTE) and the Corporation for Public Broadcasting each calls its list of metadata elements a "metadata dictionary," whereas the Dublin Core Metadata Initiative calls its list a "metadata element set" (although they are all arguably registers of terms and their definitions). MPEG-7 and MPEG-21 do not have registries of elements and definitions in the same way but instead define many elements in an extensible and dynamic way, with only a few fixed definitions, so that they can be used as a toolkit for making description schemes, each of which can have its own definition of terms.

Requirements from user communities are very different. For program research, discovery is an important factor; therefore search results must be wide enough to accommodate this requirement and there is considerable reliance on human intelligence. For technical applications, any hint of ambiguity can cause a system failure (with its resulting blank TV screens), so absolute precision is therefore essential. For many business and administrative functions, precision and confidentiality are necessary. Despite the differing requirements, as program making moves from its traditional methodologies and into the digital domain, all need to be accommodated. After all, to a digital system an invoice, script, sound track, and library catalog are all just binary data that can be transported, stored, and handled as such. Whether they make sense when they get to their end user is another matter altogether!

Because each community has developed its own systems over many years, usually in isolation, it is essential when navigating metadata systems from the various communities to be clear on definitions of terms, as each system will have been developed with different applications in mind. Frequently, too, shortcuts will have been taken because the syntax and semantic for a given application or community is known and, *within that community,* unambiguous. This means that mapping between systems can be, to say the least, interesting: a system developed for precision will often map easily to one developed for research or discovery—though several "precise" elements will map to a single "discovery" element. The reverse mapping will always be ambiguous, with several possibilities which can arise, for example, when mapping between the SMPTE Metadata Dictionary with its more than 1,700 data elements and the Dublin Core Set with its basic 15 elements. Clearly, a "round loop trip" from one system to another and then back again is unlikely to end up back at the starting point—this is a real problem in any end-to-end digital system. It is possible too that what is considered elemental in one system is not really elemental at all. For example, an element called "program title" might actually tell you two things: that you are dealing with a title (a sort of identifier) and that it is associated with a complete program. Similarly, "series title" also tells you two things: one is that you are dealing with a title, the other that it is associated with a series rather than an individual program. In other words, "program title" and "series title" are really metadata sets that combine an identifier type (title) with a sort of metadata adjective (program, series). Be careful here, though—the rules that have to be followed when encoding metadata or writing a program involving metadata can impose a strict discipline as to exactly how to deal with these apparently simple sets.

Grouping (sets) of metadata elements, or of elements and descriptors, can be considered to be a list of standardized metadata "sentences" or "phrases," which can be passed across system interfaces and which will therefore be understood with no semantic ambiguity by the systems on either side of an interface. In the same way that a natural language uses brackets, metadata groups can be nested within one another. In other words, a group can contain within it another group and so on—theoretically, ad infinitum (though most standards restrict the depth of such nesting).

It is entirely possible (and indeed likely) that on either side of the interface, the metadata elements contained in a standard metadata group presented at an interface will be mapped in some proprietary way within the boundaries of that system to suit its internal workings. The important issue is that, at a system boundary and interface, there is a standardized presentation of the metadata. What a "black box" system does with metadata for its own internal workings is of no interest to the standard, which describes what happens at the system interface, and neither should it be. This point cannot be emphasized too strongly.

Object Records and Item Records (Complex Objects)

Before delving into specific standards for data structures, rules, and values, we should discuss the concept of object records and their related item-level records. The library science community terms this cataloging *complex objects*. Understanding complex objects is key to cataloging moving image materials, where the main work (program) can have several versions, with each version having several physical and digital elements or items associated to it (AB rolls on film, air version on tape, music tracks on audio, etc.). All of the individual items must link to the master record. In databases, this can mean that the master record only need be created once, a version record also created once, and item records can be as many as needed.

The International Federation of Library Associations and Institutions (IFLA) (www.ifla.org) outlined the concept of complex objects in its "Functional Requirements for Bibliographic Records" (FRBR) in 1998.[1] Moving image archives had already been grappling with this concept for years but did not have a name for it. FRBR outlines four distinct parts of a catalog record for a complex object: work, expression, manifestation, and item.

- The *work* is the "intellectual or artistic creation." It is what is owned in intellectual property: not a physical object, but the creative work that is put down in tangible form. With broadcasting and moving image materials, it describes the original release version of the work. Metadata at the "work" level would include descriptive metadata about the work's creation (title, personnel, summaries, subjects, and genres), identification (a unique alphanumeric for the program that could well have been assigned at the idea development stage), and administrative/legal information.
- The *expression* is a variation of the work. These data also describe the intellectual property or content of the expression (variation) rather than a physical piece. The expression could be the original release version, or it could be a version that has been edited, subtitled, presented with a different ending, and so on. Metadata for the expression would include metadata for the work, as

---

[1] www.ifla.org/VII/s13/frbr/frbr.pdf.

well as additional information identifying the version. The record would also include a unique identifier for the particular expression, still linking it to the master "work" record.

- The *manifestation* is "the physical embodiment of an expression of a work." For example, a program could exist on film, video, and digital file. The metadata would describe the physical manifestation of the expression. It too would have a unique identifier, linking it to the metadata for the work and expression.
- An *item* is also a physical piece. Here is where the cataloger would note the kind of element: is it the picture negative for the film manifestation, the master tape for the air version, or the MP3 file of the music track?

Moving image catalogers take the complex object concept a bit further. Often an organization will want to link together all works related to a program. For example, trailers, commercials, publicity stills, scripts, and posters would be linked to the program they support. Supporting items such as these are called "documentation." Here, the documentation would be linked in the database or digital asset management system by the work's and expression's unique identifiers.

Metadata Structure Standards

As described in Chapter 1, a metadata structure is the overall record structure for all records in the database. It can be a list of fields acting as a metadata dictionary, or a scheme that shows relationships between data elements. The broadcasting, library, and archival communities have developed data structure standards relevant for broadcasting. Several of them are described in this section. The fact that there are so many "standards" could imply that there aren't any standards; there isn't one data structure that all users follow. Users tend to select what is best for their purposes, often picking and choosing between the structures to create their own internal standard. Users following this approach should at least be familiar with the different "standards" in use in the field and create a mapping to relevant structures in preparation for any possible interoperating in the future.

Broadcast Industry Standards

Society of Motion Picture and Television Engineers (SMPTE)
www.smpte-ra.org/mdd/index.html

The SMPTE started work on the handling of metadata following the publication of the "EBU/SMPTE* Task Force for Harmonised Standards for the Exchange of Programme Material as Bitstreams" in 1998.

---

* European Broadcasting Union, based in Geneva.

Work started on an SMPTE Metadata Dictionary (or Register of Metadata Elements, RP210) at about the same time. The need for precision in handling and interchanging technical metadata quickly led to the realization that in a fully digital system there was a need to agree upon standard groupings of metadata elements from this dictionary in order to both preserve the correct syntax or semantic meaning and enable standardization of interfaces between systems and databases. It was realized at that time that it would be necessary to agree on the data types that were to be used—for instance, whether a text string should be represented as ASCII or Unicode where each is a different representation of the same text but it is essential for users to know which is being used.

The SMPTE Metadata Dictionary is defined by SMPTE Standard 335M and has been standardized as Recommended Practice 210. It is regularly updated by the addition of new metadata elements (deletions are not permitted in order to give some degree of future-proofing and backward compatibility). Currently, more than 1,700 elements are listed in the dictionary. Each entry is uniquely registered so that it can be unambiguously referenced. Unlike the Dublin Core and PBCore work, there are no qualifiers listed separately from the SMPTE Metadata Dictionary—the dictionary is effectively a register of all data items including those that Dublin Core and PBCore would regard as qualifiers or modifiers and list separately. This gives great flexibility in making up metadata "sentences," since it is effectively simply a list of all possible metadata "words," each uniquely entered in a register, which can be used to construct metadata "sentences"—some are "nouns," some "adjectives," "adverbs," "verbs," and so on. In simple terms, these metadata "sentences" *are* the metadata groups and sets to which we have already referred.

For management purposes, entries in the SMPTE Metadata Dictionary are grouped under a number of "nodes"—identifiers and locators, administration, interpretive, parametric, process, spacio-temporal, and experimental. There are also nodes for elements registered for public use by user organizations and elements registered as private by user organizations for their own use. An extract from the SMPTE Metadata Dictionary is presented in Appendix 2.

The SMPTE Groups Register, as outlined earlier, contains a list of uniquely registered groups (or sets) of metadata elements used in systems and is defined by SMPTE359M. Each group (or set) can be unambiguously identified at an interface or exchange point, so that a receiving system will know exactly what to expect, what the group contains, and how the metadata is represented because each element within the group will have a known datatype. Note that some SMPTE standards predate the groups register and have their own lists of groups to be used (the Material eXchange Format is one such standard); however, there should be no conflict as these groups are duplicated in the groups register.

At the time of this writing, the SMPTE is in the early stages of starting work on a controlled vocabulary register. This register will list the controlled terms that can be used with metadata elements where the values permitted are an enumerated list. More on this effort is discussed later.

The last SMPTE register is the labels register, which is defined by SMPTE400M and standardized as Recommended Practice 224. This is a specialized list of enumerated or controlled terms used mainly to label audio or video data. A label is a specialized and unique identifier that is attached to the video or audio data it identifies—in other words, it labels audio or video data with what it is: MPEG*, uncompressed video, AES† audio, and so on. In much the same way as clothing labels function in a store, when a piece of identification metadata is attached to that which it identifies, it becomes a label.

Although originally intended for use in key-length-value (KLV) encoded system, the use of the registries is not restricted to KLV. They can be used equally well with XML encodings, several of which are being developed at the time of this writing.

Entries in the SMPTE Metadata Dictionary (or Register of Metadata Elements) can be used in conjunction with groups, types, labels, and controlled vocabularies to build descriptive metadata schemes. The SMPTE publishes an engineering guideline on how to do this—EG42. There is also the Descriptive Metadata Scheme (DMS-1) standard (SMPTE380M), which was constructed using that guideline and intended for use with the Material eXchange Format (MXF). Care is needed when using DMS-1, as it relies heavily on the underlying structure of the MXF file format. Nevertheless it can contain many of the descriptive metadata elements commonly encountered in program making and archiving. The full scheme is large and rich—it has three frameworks, each with many groups and each group comprising several elements. However, almost all of these components are optional and can simply be omitted if they are not required. The three frameworks are for production, scene, and clip metadata: production metadata is overall metadata that applies to the whole program; scene metadata describes conceptual and editorial information (e.g., where a depicted scene is supposed to be, not where it was actually shot); clip information describes factual information about the capture of the essence (e.g., where a depicted scene was actually shot, not where it is supposed to be). An extract from DMS-1 is presented in Appendix 2.

European Broadcasting Union P/Meta
www.ebu.ch/en/technical/metadata/specifications/notes_on_tech3295.php

The European Broadcasting Union (EBU) has member broadcasters throughout Europe and a large and complex network for exchanging program material between members from the north coast of Africa to Scandinavia and the eastern Mediterranean to Portugal and Ireland. The exchanges range from news material

---

* Motion Picture Experts Group.
† Audio Engineering Society.

to sports to light entertainment, drama, and classical music. In addition, members exchange program material using the traditional tape reel or cassette transported physically by road or air. However, the advantages of transferring programs electronically are plain.

Consequently, the need for some form of standard for the exchange of metadata was identified. Work to establish a standard started in 1999, informed to some extent by work already in progress at the British Broadcasting Corporation (BBC) on its Standard Media Exchange Format (SMEF) and similar work at Radiotelevisione Italiana (RAI) in Italy.

Similarly to the SMPTE work, P/Meta consists of a flat list (i.e., it is unstructured) of metadata items intended for business-to-business use when exchanging programs along with standard metadata groups and lists of controlled terms. P/Meta has syntactical rules, which must be followed when constructing metadata groups, although it does have some hidden groups within its list of elements in that some P/Meta elements can be split into smaller parts.

Institut für Rundfunktechnik GmbH (IRT)
www.irt.de/IRT/home/indexbmf_e.htm

The IRT is the central research and development establishment of the Public Broadcasters in Germany (ARD, ZDF, DLR), as well as for Austria's ORF, and Switzerland's SRG/SSR.

At the time of this writing, work is well advanced on researching and constructing a comprehensive model (the Broadcast Metadata Exchange Format [BMEF]) of the metadata used in those organizations and how the individual metadata elements relate to each other. The results are not yet public but have some commonality with the SMPTE's descriptive metadata work, both in terms of the individual metadata elements used and the grouping involved. The IRT has a website for BMEF at the preceding link.

Motion Picture Experts Group MPEG-7
www.chiariglione.org/mpeg/standards/mpeg-7/mpeg-7.htm

MPEG-7 is an International Standards Organisation/International Electrotechnical Commission (ISO/IEC) standard developed by the Moving Picture Experts Group (MPEG) in Joint Technical Committee1/Sub-Committee 29/Working Group11 (or ISO/IEC JTC1/SC29/WG11 for short). It is a scheme rather than a dictionary, since it shows relationships between data elements. It was not specifically developed for program making and has a general application, though there is a broadcast profile.

The goal of the MPEG-7 standard is to allow searching, indexing, filtering, and access of audiovisual content across separate and diverse systems by enabling

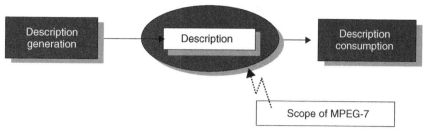

Figure 3.1.

interoperability among devices and applications that deal with AV content descriptions. MPEG-7 descriptions take two possible forms: a textual XML form suitable for editing, searching, and filtering and a binary form suitable for storage, transmission, and streaming delivery, thus allowing both full textual descriptions and concise, machine-generated descriptions.

The standard specifies four sorts of normative components: descriptors, description schemes (DSs), a description definition language (DDL), and coding schemes.

The MPEG-7 descriptors primarily describe low-level audio or visual features such as color, texture, motion, audio energy, and so forth, as well as some of the more usual text-based attributes of AV content such as location, time, and quality. As new technology develops, applications will automatically extract descriptors for low-level features (Figure 3.1).

Both human users and automated systems that process audiovisual information are within the scope of the MPEG-7 standard, formally called the "Multimedia Content Description Interface," the object of which is to provide a rich set of standardized tools that will enable users to describe multimedia content. MPEG-7 facilitates the creation of such tools in a standardized way, so that consistent results are obtained when the tools are applied, irrespective of the system or application—in other words, MPEG-7 is not used directly to create descriptions, but rather to produce the tools that create the description. It is important to appreciate that this "level of indirection" is involved when using the MPEG-7 standard.

The MPEG-7 toolsets can be used for all kinds of content description and can be used both for Internet multimedia applications or broadcast consumer applications and for the professional production domain. The complete toolset can also be used to create a profile/subset that is exactly tailored to match a specific implementation of an application. This capability can be seen as a strong point, but at the same time it can be a weak point since in most cases a significant amount of time is necessary to "profile" the toolset and produce the tools themselves for a particular application.

The MPEG-7 standard is far reaching and broad in scope, and many tools are available to describe individual objects within a frame. The system can be used in real-time and in non-real-time applications, and the output can be embedded in the content or stored in a separate database.

MPEG-7 has been used for projects in education,[2] media (electronic news or news-papers), culture, entertainment, geography, and medicine, among other fields. The standard does not have technical constraints and all analog, digital, or even paper-based systems can use it. However, it is worth mentioning that MPEG-7 lends itself particularly well to MPEG-4 object coding techniques.

In any system or application, descriptions have to be meaningful, and this usually implies that knowledge of the context in which the description is made is important. It follows that different user communities or different applications will describe the same material in different ways. Descriptions for use in a library will be broad in context, require a high level of semantic input, and probably need human intelligence to derive them, whereas structural descriptors used within a digital file format are defined in a tight context at low level and probably are invisible to any user. In between these extremes are descriptors that are analytical in nature—shape, size, texture, position, trajectory, timbre, tempo, and so on. Across such a broad range of contexts, clearly some descriptors will need considerable human interaction with any system, some will be closely defined by the application, and others can be extracted automatically by the application.

The Major Components of MPEG-7

The standard consists of a bundle of tools, which together form the toolset:

MPEG-7 systems. These tools support binary coded representation for efficient storage and transmission (widely known as BiM encoding), transmission mechanisms (both for textual and binary formats), multiplexing of descriptions, synchronization of descriptions with content, management and protection of intellectual property in MPEG-7 descriptions, and so on.

MPEG-7 description definition language—(DDL). Based on XML Schema, but with specific MPEG-7 extensions, DDL defines the syntax of the MPEG-7 description tools to allow the creation of new description schemes and, possibly, descriptors. It also allows the extension and modification of existing description schemes.

MPEG-7 visual. These tools deal with visual descriptions covering basic visual features like color, texture, shape, motion, localization, and face recognition.

MPEG-7 audio. These description tools deal with audio features (such as the spectral, parametric, or temporal characteristics of a signal) and sound recognition, timbre, melody, and spoken content.

---

[2] An example of MPEG-7 used in the public archive and educational community is the Moving Image Collections (MIC) database (http://mic.imtc.gatech.edu/), which maps data from MPEG-7 and MARC.

MPEG-7 multimedia description schemes. The descriptors (D) that define the syntax and the semantics of each feature (metadata element), and the description schemes (DS) that specify the structure and semantics of the relationships between their components (which may be both descriptors and description schemes).

These schemes make it possible to use audiovisual content descriptions and content management for searching, indexing, filtering, and access, and they may be generic to all media or complex when more than one medium is being described (e.g., audio and video together).

Description tools can be grouped into five different classes according to their functionality:

Content description. Representation of perceivable information

Content management. Information about the media features, the creation, and the usage of the AV content

Content organization. Representation of the analysis and classification of several AV contents

Navigation and access. Specification of summaries and variations of the AV content

User interaction. Description of user preferences and usage history pertaining to the consumption of the multimedia material

The testing tools are as follows:

MPEG-7 reference software. A software implementation of relevant parts of the MPEG-7 standard with normative status

MPEG-7 conformance testing. Guidelines and procedures for testing conformance of MPEG-7 implementations

There are also application guidelines:

MPEG-7 extraction and use of descriptions. Informative material (in the form of a technical report) about the extraction and use of some of the description tools

MPEG-7 profiles and levels. Provide guidelines and standard profiles; current profiles concentrate on the description definition language, visual, audio, and multimedia description schemes that are based on the namespace versioning defined in schema definition

MPEG-7 schema definition. Specifies the schema using the description definition language and collects all the MPEG-7 schemas from the different parts of the standard as well as from corrigenda and amendments

Motion Picture Experts Group MPEG-21

www.chiariglione.org/mpeg/standards/mpeg-21/mpeg-21.htm

At the time of this writing, MPEG-21 is not yet completed. Like MPEG-7, it is a scheme rather than a metadata dictionary.

Work on the MPEG-21 framework began in 1999 within the MPEG community and has been driven mainly by the motivation to develop mechanisms for intellectual property management and protection. The MPEG-21 group considers that this will become more and more important in a world where every kind of content can be produced by almost any individual. The group anticipates that the borderline between private individuals as content providers and the professional production companies will blur over a relatively short time. As technology advances, it will become possible for every consumer to produce content to share with others but at the same time identify as their own and protect in intellectual terms. This is part of an inexorable move toward an integrated and harmonized global environment.

MPEG-21 is not a metadata standard as such; it is a *framework* that makes extensive use of metadata and provides a controlled environment for content creators and users to exchange content and the ownership of constraints governing the use of that content.

Probably the most important metadata structure within MPEG-21 is the digital item, which both defines and describes content using a set of metadata elements and is, in effect, the digital representation of an audiovisual asset (the content plus the rights to use it). This definition of the item is called the digital item declaration. The digital item is the fundamental digital object for transactions and distribution. Users access the metadata within it to find out what the item is (audio, video, graphic, text, etc.), the owner of the content, and how to use the content in a legal way.

The goal of MPEG-21 is to achieve interoperability on a "best effort" basis between devices or systems (which inevitably use a variety of other standards or frameworks) and to achieve the highest possible level of automation in operation. In consequence, MPEG-21 involves technical infrastructure, security, rights management, secure payment methodologies, and so on.

It follows that one objective of the MPEG-21 developers has been to achieve the highest possible level of interoperability with other standards. To achieve this, the MPEG-21 group interacts with a long list of working groups or standardization bodies that work in the field of multimedia identification and metadata. On a regular basis, MPEG-21 provides technical reports that explain the completed work, work in progress, and standard implementation. A major commitment in the overall MPEG standardization process is to always make conformance testing tools available. MPEG-21 is no exception.

The MPEG-21 framework contains different domains of metadata use:

- Metadata that describes the content both in terms of its production and of the final interaction between the user and the content.
- Metadata that can be used for the exchange of content and for optimizing that content.
- Metadata that describes the rights and permitted usage of the content.

The metadata for optimization of the exchange is used in a highly automated process between the service provider and the user's device. This is highly specialized metadata and is outside the scope of this book, as is the rights metadata and other metadata about the conditions and permissions involved in using the content.

An XML schema has been defined to create the digital item descriptions. In the schema, the main building blocks of the description are defined using the relevant MPEG-7 elements and options to construct complete digital items.

Corporation for Public Broadcasting PBCore
www.utah.edu/cpbmetadata

The Corporation for Public Broadcasting (CPB) in the United States has created what it calls a metadata dictionary with the goal of providing a simple structure that its member stations can share. The CPB needed a metadata structure that could incorporate records, not only from its productions but also related materials such as books, DVDs, and CD-ROMs. After reviewing the available or developing broadcasting and library standards such as the BBC's SMEF-DM, MPEG-7, and MARC (described later), the CPB decided that those metadata structures required either too advanced cataloging skills or were too narrowly focused on broadcasting and could not encompass their other media types.

Based on Dublin Core (described later), PBCore offers 48 main elements and subelements. A subelement is a descriptor closely associated with a main element in much the same way as Dublin Core uses qualifiers (e.g., the publisher's name is a main element and publisherRole is an associated or subelement). The elements fall into three categories:

- *Content.* Thirteen elements describing the intellectual content of the work (in FRBR, the "work" and "expression")
- *Intellectual property.* Seven elements describing the creators of the work (personnel) and business/legal metadata
- *Instantiation.* Twenty-eight elements describing the physical or digital item (in FRBR, the "manifestation" and "item")

The instantiation elements include fields for digital technical information such as Format.DataRate. However, the fields are more general and not as extensive as in the SMPTE Metadata Dictionary, which is geared toward engineers to help them store, manage, and playout digital files. PBCore is more useful for managing assets in a distributed library catalog.

PBCore is available as a free license. The full list of fields and their definitions can be found at www.utah.edu/cpbmetadata/PBCore/UserGuide.html. Sample PBCore records from Wisconsin Public Television and Kentucky Educational Television (KET) can be found in Appendix 1.

British Broadcasting Corporation Standard Media Exchange Framework (SMEF)
www.bbc.co.uk/guidelines/smef

> The BBC has created a comprehensive data model for the enterprise-wide management of its media assets. Called the Standard Media Exchange Framework Data Model (SMEF-DM), it can be applied for an end-to-end description of media assets, from creation to distribution. This is a large piece of work and covers all metadata, both technical and descriptive. The number of data entries is correspondingly large, both in terms of the elements themselves and the groupings involved. SMEF-DM is available as a free license.

Press Industry Standard

International Press Telecommunications Council (IPTC) NewsML
www.iptc.org

> The International Press Telecommunications Council has developed NewsML, a specialized metadata exchange format for the interchange of news content between the world's press organizations. The standard is part of a suite of specialized press standards for all news and sports programs (see also the section on metadata value standards discussed later). It is in use worldwide for the exchange of news items between editorial systems, news agencies, publishers, news aggregators, news service providers, and end users. The complete list of participating companies can be found at www.iptc.org/pages/index.php and www.newsml.org/pages/index.php.

> NewsML was developed as an open standard in response to the continuing growth in electronic techniques for the use and reuse of news stories throughout the world, with the rapid expansion of the Internet being a strong driving force. News items can point to a variety of different media—such as text, photographs, graphics, video, and audio—although, optionally, the content can be embedded in the file alongside the metadata.

> NewsML is designed to provide a media-independent XML-based structural framework for multimedia news. It can be applied at all stages in the electronic news life cycle including editorial systems, news exchange, archiving, publishing, and end users.

Library Standards

Dublin Core Metadata Initiative
www.dublincore.org

> The Dublin Core metadata element set was developed beginning in 1995 by a group of librarians and digital information specialists in the United States, and it has been approved as a U.S. National Standard (ANSI/NISO Z39.85). It is essentially a list of simplified metadata fields that can be applied across many formats; it is not

locked into a particular media type. There are no fundamental restrictions to the types of resources to which Dublin Core metadata can be assigned; they can be used to describe digital assets, images, books, films, and broadcast materials.

The element set (which as of this writing has remained unchanged since 1999) contains 15 basic descriptive elements, each of which can be modified by a "qualifier" as described earlier in this chapter. Each descriptive element, along with its qualifiers, can occur many times—for instance, if there is more than one "contributor" to a program, there will effectively be a list of contributor elements, each with its qualifier defining the role of that contributor. In practice, each element frequently "labels" a free text entry, which can be very long with one entry containing a mixture of textual information—easy enough for human intelligence to sort out, but quite often ambiguous to a computer.

Dublin Core has been most successfully applied in metadata structures that are simple, or as a means to translate an organization's internal complex information to outside users. That is not to say that complex objects such as broadcasting materials cannot be described in a Dublin Core–influenced structure. For example, the PBCore initiative was based on Dublin Core and should be carefully followed to monitor its maturation as it adapts to users' experiences.

Library of Congress MARC 21
www.loc.gov/marc

MARC is an acronym for Machine-Readable Cataloging and is the data structure for cataloging used by the vast majority of libraries in the United States and Canada. Developed by the Library of Congress in the 1960s, it became the standard for inputting records for all formats in library online catalogs. Because of its specific and well-defined field and subfield structure, it allows for easy sharing of catalog information by libraries that use MARC for cataloging. Archives holding broadcasting material that are associated with university and public libraries tend to catalog in MARC format since their parent organization (the library) uses MARC in cataloging more traditional holdings (books, periodicals, etc.). The latest version of MARC is called MARC 21.

MARC has these basic categories:

0XX	Unique identifiers (control information, numbers, codes)
1XX	Main entry (name of creator)
2XX	Title (in general, the title, statement of responsibility, edition, and publication information)
3XX	Physical description and so on
4XX	Series
5XX	Notes (includes preservation and legal information)
6XX	Subjects and genres
7XX	Names of personnel

There are hundreds of fields within these larger categories. The advantage of the fields and subfields structure is that like the SMPTE Metadata Dictionary, data can be unambiguously analyzed and exported. Public archives that catalog their holdings in MARC also have the benefit of being able to share information about their collections with millions of users around the world through shared bibliographic utilities such as the Online Computer Library Center (OCLC).[3] For an example of a MARC record of an entertainment broadcasting title, see the UCLA Film and Television Archive sample record in Appendix 1.

Archival Standards

International Federation of Television Archives (FIAT/IFTA)
www.fiatifta.org

The International Federation of Television Archives is an association of national and broadcast archives and libraries. In 1992, it published a minimum data list of 22 fields for cataloging broadcast materials. This predates the era of digital production, but the list can still serve a purpose as a kind of expanded Dublin Core. There are three main areas, although the areas sometimes overlap:

- *Identification.* Eight fields that combine identification, descriptive, and limited personnel information; this category also includes date of shooting and date of transmission
- *Technical.* Nine fields that include physical description of the item but also include some information that could be in the descriptive area (content, keywords, place of shooting)
- *Legal.* Five fields that describe who own rights to the work and where it was acquired if not produced by the organization; this category also includes more extensive personnel information in the context of persons with specific rights

The list of metadata elements is available through the FIAT website at www.fiatifta.org/projects/standards/#metadata, but access is for FIAT members only.

Independent Media Arts Preservation (IMAP)
www.imappreserve.org

While this group is primarily concerned with independent video works and their preservation, they have created a cataloging tool that automatically translates a record between MARC and Dublin Core, which could be useful for all genres of moving images. The IMAP's cataloging template is not a standard in itself, but it utilizes standards and mappings in a way that simplifies the cataloging process.

---

[3] The Online Computer Library Center (OCLC) is the primary cataloging database and tool for public and higher education libraries in the United States and Canada. Libraries catalog their records in MARC directly into OCLC, and the records are automatically shared with fellow OCLC subscribers at the same time the record is added to the library's own online catalog.

The metadata structure is based on MARC fields, although the field labels on the main screen are in common language rather than MARC numeric tags. The structure is divided into these areas:

- Unique identifiers (location on shelf, accession numbers, etc.)
- Title and intellectual description
- Physical description (a tab takes the user to fields for audio, film, or video, depending on the item being cataloged)
- Acquisition, usage, and restrictions (how the organization acquired the work, copyright and usage terms, preservation actions)
- Intellectual access (personnel and genre)
- Subjects
- Local information (address of the organization, cataloger name)

In the catalog record example on IMAP's website, the immediate mapping of rich MARC data to the Dublin Core record shows the loss of information during the transformation.

Metadata Rules Standards

If metadata structures provide the architecture for the data, then the metadata rules are the guidelines for the format in how the data should be entered within specific fields. The broadcasting industry has not created a standard for rules; the only two that exist in the English-speaking countries were created by standards bodies in the library community.

Anglo-American Cataloguing Rules (AACR2)

Anglo-American Cataloguing Rules[4] were first published in 1967 as a set of standardized rules to create descriptive metadata for books, serials, moving images, and other media. A second edition was published in 1978, with most recent revisions published in 2004. The AACR Joint Steering Committee (2005) is reviewing additions to AACR3.

The rules are established by library associations in English-speaking countries: the United States, the United Kingdom, and Canada. Most public and academic libraries in these countries use these rules. Chapter 7 on moving image materials provides basic guidance for cataloging published works (commercial tapes, DVDs, etc.) but is limited in its experience for archival or broadcasting materials. Because of this shortcoming, the Library of Congress in the United States created a separate set of standards for describing archival and broadcasting moving

---

[4] *Anglo-American Cataloguing Rules,* Second Edition, 2002 Revision: 2004 Update, prepared by the American Library Association, the Canadian Library Association, and the Chartered Institute of Library and Information Professionals. Chicago: American Library Association, 2004.

images that is based on AACR2 (AMIM2, described next). However, the rules in AACR2 do provide helpful information in standardizing the structure of names, which can help in creating internal standardized name authority lists.

For example, the rules state that last names beginning with "Van" should place the "van" *after* the main word in the name. With this rule, the name "Vincent van Gogh" would be entered as

Gogh, Vincent van

   not as

Van Gogh, Vincent

Archival Moving Image Materials, Version 2 (AMIM2)

The Motion Picture, Broadcasting, and Recorded Sound Division at the Library of Congress developed *Archival Moving Image Materials*[5] as a descriptive standard for cataloging archival moving images such as commercial films, television and broadcasting programs, home movies, and oral histories. Built on top of AACR2 and first published in 1986, it was revised as AMIM2 in 2000. AMIM2 includes sample records with MARC field tags. This standard is primarily used by university-based archives in the United States, although AMIM2's enhanced television cataloging section would be of interest to commercial broadcasters.

Metadata Value Standards

Using Controlled Vocabularies and Thesauri

Metadata values are the actual words and numbers contained in the fields (structure) according to proscribed rules. *Controlled vocabularies* should be used as values wherever possible to maintain consistency in inputting and retrieval. A controlled vocabulary is a list of terms or names that cluster variants of a term or name around a preferred heading. In broadcasting, controlled vocabularies can most often be found supplying authorized terms for names, genres, subjects, and media formats.

While there are several standardized controlled vocabularies created by various organizations, most broadcasters use internal lists. Internal lists are fine; the key is to use them consistently. In broadcasting, footage usually has to be found immediately. Poor application of controlled lists means that footage will not be found or will be found with difficulty.

If a database or digital asset management system (DAM) is able to search thesauri, the cataloger's work is easier. With a thesaurus functionality, a user can type the phrase "American Civil War" and retrieve all records cataloged with subject

---

[5] AMIM2 can be purchased from the Library of Congress' website: www.loc.gov/cds/catman.html.

headings "Civil War (United States)," "War between the States," and "War of Yankee Aggression." (Of course, no records claiming to represent actual footage of the war should be found since it ended in 1865!)

Thesauri can make it unnecessary for the cataloger inputting the metadata to have to worry about using the standardized, authorized term. This is because all related terms will be searched in a query. However, retrieval depends on staff adding all possible terms to the thesaurus in advance. A library science professional should supervise the thesaurus creation and maintain the list.

As footage and programs are shared across international borders, metadata describing the programs become very important so that people whose native language and culture are not the same as the producing entity's can still find what they need. Users will need to find content on particular topics that could be named differently according to the native culture (e.g., "revolution" or "war of liberation," "murder" or "killings") and also search for footage with specific shots or technical specifications. The latter task would be the least difficult to achieve. Dictionaries of broadcasting terms can be found comparing a few languages (English, French, and German, for example), but a true international standard thesaurus of broadcasting terminologies has not yet been created. The process of writing this very book is a good example of why such a thesaurus is needed. The three co-authors come from three countries: the United Kingdom, the United States, and the Netherlands. While English was the common writing language, the authors found themselves asking the others to define many of the broadcasting terms and production slang they used in their own sections.

A broadcasting terminology dictionary would be easy to create in comparison to creating thesauri and controlled vocabularies for content. In both cases, cultural differences as well as language must be addressed. Consumer metadata for video on demand created by the original broadcasting network in its own country might not read as well in a different culture. This problem can be easily solved: the broadcaster in the licensing country can write its own copy. More difficult is when researchers purchase footage with its corresponding metadata from another broadcaster and add it to their own libraries for producers to use. The original metadata might not make any sense to the purchasing broadcaster, and as a result the footage may not be retrieved. Creating an international thesaurus of major global events would be a good start. Dictionaries of nouns in different languages and cultures already exist and would need to be applied on top of a digital asset management or cataloging system.

International Press Telecommunications Council (IPTC)
www.iptc.org

The IPTC standard originated as file header metadata for digital still images used in the press and is one of the suites of standards that includes NewsML (discussed earlier). It has expanded to include controlled vocabularies for approximately 1,300 subject terms that could be useful for broadcast news–based metadata (see the list of subject terms posted at www.iptc.org/NewsCodes/nc_ts-table01.php). The list includes definitions for political, cultural, entertainment, and sports events and provides definitions. The terms can be broad (e.g., "politics—general"), or narrow, especially in the case of sports ("50-m hurdles"). Given the generality of the terms, catalogers choosing to use the IPTC standards would probably use them as a starting point, adding terms from other controlled vocabularies or their organizations' own internal lists. Note that this list is only in English. An example of a broadcaster applying IPTC subject headings is the sample record from Wisconsin Public Television in Appendix 1.

Library of Congress Name Authority File (LCNAF)
http://authorities.loc.gov/

The Library of Congress is responsible for maintaining two important controlled vocabularies: the Library of Congress Name Authority File (LCNAF) and the Library of Congress Subject Headings (LCSH, described next). The LCNAF holds millions of names and their authorized forms and variants. Most libraries in the United States use the LCNAF for authorized forms of personal and corporate names. Thousands of names relating to broadcasting have been added since the mid-1990s, as libraries began more vigorously cataloging their television and broadcasting holdings. While name authority records are created in MARC format, the MARC tags can easily be ignored to find the needed information.

Using the Vincent van Gogh example mentioned earlier, if one searches the LCNAF for "Van Gogh, Vincent," two similar headings are displayed:

Van Gogh, Vincent, 1820–1888

Van Gogh, Vincent, 1853–1890

When names are similar, they must be distinguished in some way to make them unique. Life dates are often appended to the names to distinguish them. If dates are not known, then often a relator term is added to the name: director, artist, actor, and so on.

In the Van Gogh example, clicking on the first Vincent brings up the authorized form of the name: Gogh, Vincent van, 1820–1888. The name authority record tells us that this Vincent was uncle to the artist Vincent.

Television and broadcasting stations and production companies are also included in the LCNAF as corporate names. These authorized records can be very useful as they give the history of a station and its often-changing call letters. For example, the authorized record for "WNET," the public broadcasting station in New York City, provides this useful information:

670 __ |**a** E-mail from station WNET, Apr. 01, 1999 |**b** (call letters changed from WNDT to WNET in 1970, with the merger of WNDT and NET [National Educational Television]. WNDT chartered in NJ in 1962. NET did majority of national programming, was based in New York City. Thirteen/WNET owns copyright on all WNDT and NET programs produced before 1970)

LCNAF is available through cataloging bibliographic utilities such as OCLC or for purchase. It is also available free on the Internet at authorities.loc.gov. An example of a public archive using LCNAF headings can be found in the UCLA Film and Television Archive's record in Appendix 1.

Library of Congress Subject Headings (LCSH)
http://authorities.loc.gov

What the LCNAF does for names, the Library of Congress Subject Headings (LCSH) does for subjects and geographic areas. The LCSH provides authorized forms of subjects, with references to other forms of a heading.

An example of an authorized form of a heading is a search for "Vietnam War." The authorized form of this topic is "Vietnamese Conflict, 1961–1975." Similar forms of the heading are included in the authority record for cross-references:

Vietnam War, 1961–1975

Vietnamese War, 1961–1975

Vietnam Conflict, 1961–1975

Most libraries and archives attached to public universities or institutions in the United States assign LCNAF and LCSH to their MARC catalog records. However, LCSH's broad terms can provide a ready-made, controlled vocabulary for catalogers working in a broadcasting environment.

LCSH is available as a package with the LCNAF through the free URL mentioned previously or for purchase through OCLC or the Library of Congress. An example of a public archive using LCNAF headings can be found in the UCLA Film and Television Archive's record in the appendices.

Moving Image Genre-Form Guide
www.loc.gov/rr/mopic/migintro.html

The genre or form of a work is not its subject, but rather a word or brief phrase describing the general type of work. Examples include Science fiction, Western, Soap opera, and News. Noting the genre of a work in its metadata is useful for programming, scheduling, and video-on-demand purposes.

Genre lists are usually created internally at broadcasting organizations, but the staff at the Library of Congress has created a list that library and archive catalogers use to describe television and film works in their collections. The list includes definitions of the terms, examples, and related terms. It is freely available at the URL mentioned earlier.

Maintenance of Metadata

Metadata can be kept in many places. When files are being transferred from one place to another, then it makes sense to wrap the metadata along with the video and audio; this is particularly important for technical metadata, because without doing so, it may not be possible to play the file. Gone are the days when a simple label on the can combined with the shape of the cassette or size of film were enough information to tell users what sort of machine would play the tape. It makes sense to transfer any descriptive metadata and the program material to which it relates at the same time, preferably "stuck together" in one file. However, within a studio facility, having descriptive or business metadata stored only wrapped up in a file has its drawbacks—for searching, a database will provide easier and faster access.

It is likely then that metadata can and will be in at least two places at the same time. The metadata in a database is likely to be more used and more up to date than that wrapped up in an archived file—so care is clearly needed to make sure that any necessary mirroring is carried out before the archived file is used or transferred somewhere else.

To make matters worse, although nearly all technical metadata is fixed and unchanging, some metadata changes dynamically. Ownership and access rights are good examples of changing metadata, as are contract information and names and addresses. Metadata might be added to a database sometime after the program has been completed—audience information, for example, or additional information added by a researcher using the program as a resource. And of course, some of the metadata might be just plain wrong and will need to be corrected.

Since not all metadata is used in the same community, it may not be desirable for every user to have access to the whole of the metadata: the library would not expect to have access to contractual information or personal details about a contributor. Most of the technical detail is of use only to the technical system—traditionally, the archive has had to know some technical parameters in order to determine which sort of machine to use to access the program, but this all changes with the introduction of file formats and playout from servers. The contracts department will have little interest in archival descriptions but will use metadata that is specific to a particular business arrangement.

Lastly, some metadata exists only transiently—much of this is technical and relates to the switching and routing of material as it travels through a system. However, some can be related to business (in pay-per-view systems for instance) or in services ancillary to the main program. Clearly, there is little need to store this sort of metadata once the material has passed through the system.

Encoding of Metadata

The encoding of metadata is a very technical subject and is really outside the scope of this book. However, it is worth mentioning a couple of the reasons why there are different encoding schemes and the pitfalls that may arise in consequence.

In many computer database applications, flexibility and self-contained encoding schemes have much to recommend them. Such schemes can define their own names and definitions for metadata elements as well as arrange groupings of metadata so as to preserve context and semantic meaning as metadata is transferred between databases. It follows that they have considerable flexibility in the names and definitions they use, since they are defined separately for each encoding scheme. The schemes can be text based, as in the case of XML (eXtensible Mark-up Language) so that it is to some extent human readable. Processing speed and file size are rarely issues of concern during data interchange or storage, and an error or unknown metadata element will simply cause the system to stop until the error is corrected and the system restarted. Such schemes are in common everyday use for interchanging data between databases, and when encoded into XML they are often in a form known as XML *schema*. However, great care must be taken with the choice of names and definitions and how such names and definitions are used if more than one encoding scheme is involved. It is all too easy to use the same name with a slightly different definition or to use the same name and definition in a different context. Simply picking a likely looking metadata element from one encoding scheme and using it in another without being sure of what you are about to do is asking for trouble.

But in the domain of television, files are very large indeed (even standard-definition TV file sizes can be several terabytes or more), and the rates at which data is transported and processed are very fast if good quality TV pictures and sound are to be handled in real time—such as for a live broadcast. When metadata is wrapped into the same file as pictures and sound and has to be processed at the same time as those pictures and sound (perhaps because of its relationship and relevance to it on a frame-by-frame basis), speed and accuracy become paramount. Viewers expect to see live events as they happen and similarly expect the system to recover from an error so that the program continues and does not stop and wait for a restart. Such encoding schemes call for simple and direct processing that can be done at very high speeds and for a considerable ability to recover when an error or unknown element is encountered. One such method is the SMPTE's key-length-value encoding protocol (specified in SMPTE standard 336M), where each metadata element or grouping of metadata elements is defined by a unique key. This key references the name, definition, and length of the metadata element (so that it can be skipped over if it is unrecognized or erroneous) and finally the value of the referenced metadata element. This enables processing to be fast, accurate, and have good recovery characteristics if an error is encountered. However, it does call for the availability of registers of metadata elements and groupings, and because it is not text based, it is not at all directly human-readable. File formats such as the Material eXchange Format (MXF) specified in SMPTE standard 377M make use of this sort of encoding to wrap video streams, audio streams, and metadata into a common file container. Because MXF has considerable metadata wrapping properties, it can carry entire descriptive metadata schemes within the file along with the video and audio essences and the technical metadata. An example is the SMPTE's Descriptive Metadata Scheme-1 (DMS-1) specified in SMPTE380M.

Clearly, there are many other possibilities for encoding metadata. The chosen method will always depend on the application and may, indeed, involve a combination of encoding technologies.

4 The Impact of Technology Change on People and Metadata Processes

For the better part of the past 100 years, producing a program was, by necessity, compartmentalized by virtue of the technologies, skills, and training of the people involved. Program-making people needed creative skills combined with unlimited ideas and imagination. Logistics necessitated people with organizational and negotiating skills, and business experts looked after the money. Cameras—any cameras—were a black art that needed specialist technical knowledge to make them do anything at all. Editing had to take place where the editing machinery was installed. Film needed a chemical laboratory to reveal the picture. Videotape needed experts in both mechanical and electronic engineering. Archives maintained their records on card-based systems. Publishing a TV program required immense amounts of electrical power and people who understood the mathematics of radio waves. And no stage in the process could be started until the previous stage had been completed—if a piece of material had to be worked on by two people, one could not begin until the other had finished.

But the ubiquitous personal computer is changing all that. Paper diaries are fast disappearing, as are the once commonplace typewriters. Documents are produced using a computer. Business accounts and transactions are done on a computer. Logistical information and even mail is processed on a computer. And so it goes on. Even editing and recording equipment now use computers, and the same technology is built into every camera. Material is stored in file servers, which can serve several users at the same time and can even allow work to start on a program while the incoming pictures or sound are still being recorded. End consumers rely less and less on traditional transmitters for their television viewing—instead, cable, satellite, and the Internet are used to deliver programs.

When it seems everyone is using a computer to do his or her job, the logical question to ask is, why not join all the computers up? Needless to say, it has not been as simple as that, but this "joining up" is now starting to happen at an ever increasing pace as the digital technology underpinning this new world develops.

In this new and progressively sophisticated "digital" era, the borders between function, location and time are disappearing rapidly. Almost everything can be done from every location. Who has access to what as well as who can perform which operation on material is now dictated not by the office or technical machinery but by deliberate restrictions set up by system managers. All involved in a production will have at least some knowledge of the work of others. To some extent, this has always been true, but now personnel can, at least in theory, actually do what has been the preserve of others from their own workspaces. Some key functions still call for specialized skills, but most participants in the production process will need or already have a broad range of skills and will need to know how to use a wide variety of materials and metadata as specialist job functions disappear or change. New job function profiles will appear, calling for new skills, and the people performing those functions will become multiskilled across disciplines—though each process will still only need access to its own specialized metadata.

Everyone will eventually have the capability to use all kinds of metadata and material, raw or finished, as old boundaries between pictures, sound, music, identification, and information metadata disappear. As communications and networking technology develops, distance limitations will disappear so that any workstation will potentially have access to material from anywhere in the world—instantly. A new phenomenon will be introduced in production—media management. The role of the library is already changing from that of an archival repository and maybe final resting place of old program material to that of a working repository and active source of everything the production process needs—and the role of the archivist is changing with it, to one of program media and knowledge management without which digital systems will not work. The formal management of data in an information technology (IT) infrastructure is a common discipline and accepted in the IT world as essential, but for some reason has until recently been resisted in program making. This is possibly because of a perception that keeping program material and the information about it in a desk drawer costs very little, whereas proper management of program data and information in an IT system is seen as expensive. This misconception may have its origins in the curious practice that few broadcasters put a book value on material in a library or archive, whereas they do put value on IT equipment and business information stored on it.

Accessibility is becoming the key to realizing the potential of the new technologies and hence the need to store data and to do so in an accessible, accurately managed way according to professional standards. But a good media manager can do much more than that. Automated processes can be set up to generate and capture much useful metadata, but the media manager can anticipate requirements and manipulate the metadata so that it is available when needed and also fits the chosen production format—for instance, in terms of line standards and the timely availability of metadata to a production. Many tasks are not possible with automated processes, but they tend to be the ones that are also interesting and demanding for specialized human beings. The media manager is then in the position to develop and encourage professional expertise in indexing, cataloging, and classifying content as well as in browsing, searching, and retrieving content and metadata while the machine can be left to find the shot changes or recognize where music, loud noises, voices, crowd scenes, faces, and fast movement are and note their positions. The media manager will play a crucial role in the end-to-end electronic production chain and in making sure that content and needed metadata are at the right place at the right time. If a piece of program material is not correctly placed and identified on a digital system, it might as well not be there—no one will be able to find it or even know it exists. How many times has a "lost" manuscript been "found" safely stored in a museum but unidentified anywhere in the records?

There is no doubt that media asset management systems can help in this function (generic search engines are getting better all the time and already have effective intelligent agents built in as standard). A media asset management system has to be user friendly and intuitive to production and research crews; at the same time it must be set up to meet professional knowledge management and information science standards. It should be possible for everybody involved in a program project to find the material they need for that project when they need it. Likewise it must be possible to hide the information under conditional access to make sure that nothing can be accessed or be used by the wrong people, maybe even to the extent that they will be unaware of its existence. Indeed, this is a potential problem with everyone being multiskilled across the disciplines and being able to do their jobs interchangeably.

This blurring of the demarcations between functions is already occurring in the news production environment, where the potential for multiskilling is, arguably, the greatest. For example, journalists already edit news stories and are more aware than ever before of technical capabilities and constraints. It is not unknown for journalists to preprogram the news playout system as well as write their news stories. While this seems logical, it is ironic that now expensive journalists are performing tasks for a significant part of their working time that previously were carried out by much less expensive operators. It remains to be seen if this is a less expensive way of working overall.

Unfortunately, there is something of a downside as technology rolls out. Many (maybe all) of the standards organizations that are currently working on metadata define metadata in the context of different stages in the chain between original idea and final consumption as well as for different usage and business models. One active and important area in the development of these metadata definitions is in consumer applications and the interactions between content providers and consumers. Regrettably, this content-provider-to-consumer area is rarely taken into consideration during the production stages of realizing the program and the metadata definitions associated with those stages, so there is something of a disconnect between program-making metadata and consumer metadata. In most cases, the really important and accurate information can only come from the people who made the program in the first place, and it seems obvious to collect this information and use it throughout the chain right through to consumer applications. Nevertheless, few of the current standards take account of this need for metadata migration through the entire system. The majority of the metadata generated during production is needed by a service provider to set up its service, and the same metadata is needed to communicate and negotiate between the same service provider and the consumer or to set restrictions on the use of the material. The service provider can generate only a small part of metadata that a consumer application needs—for example, technical metadata such as the transport stream information or the program metadata in that stream.

However, the situation is beginning to change and the first tentative steps along the metadata migration road are being taken, driven by projects such as TV-Anytime (discussed in more detail in Chapter 6). The bottleneck due to a lack of compatible standards will, of necessity, have to be addressed in the near future. At that point, consumer devices will possibly be capable of receiving information over more than one delivery channel, including the Internet, so that it will become technically possible to send the bulky digital audiovisual data via a traditional broadcast environment and receive the production metadata through another channel, such as the Internet, directly from the production company or team.

This is a good point to pick up some of the topics introduced in the previous chapter and look at them in more depth.

How Is Metadata Captured and Stored?

Metadata, if captured at all, has traditionally almost always been captured on paper, with the one possible exception of time-code (which is a relatively new development in practice). At the camera stage, the recording format was known by the kind of cassette, and the cassette usually carried an identifying number. If additional information were captured during a shoot, it would be written down on paper. In the planning and production offices the same was true—paper was used for everything from contracts to research notes. It was not unusual for someone to be employed for a program purely for the contents of their FiloFax/Rolodex or, more recently, their Personal Digital Assistant (PDA). Contact lists are valuable and closely guarded metadata! In the edit suite, notes were made on paper, which was slipped inside the cassette case to supplement the title and identification metadata on the label. At transmission, detail logs were kept on paper and paper was used for reporting rights and license information. Rarely did much of this paperwork reach the archive, so librarians were employed to log the program and regenerate the metadata (albeit in a form better suited to their purposes than earlier logs). Paper was cheap and reliable, but the systems surrounding its use were inefficient and prone to error and the loss of metadata.

As technology progressed, computers were introduced into the workplace, but things got little better. Although computers were used as word processors and spreadsheets were used in planning and finance applications, little metadata was transported through the production workflow: documents and spreadsheets remained locked up on a floppy disk in a desk drawer or on an office PC, with just the occasional e-mail attachment making it between workflow stages. And the FiloFax/Rolodex still reigned supreme for contact lists.

As digital systems entered the media workflow, things began to change. To a computer system, all data looks the same—documents, spreadsheets, video, and audio files are all just binary data and can be handled as such. For the first time, the possibility exists of transporting everything in the same way, right through the workflow from one end to the other, as digital data. For the first time, it is possible to capture metadata as it is generated and store it until it needs to be accessed at some other point in the workflow. Metadata can be stored in the same way as word processor documents, spreadsheets, or video and audio files—on a file server in a network, where it will be subject to all the normal IT processes of backing up, access security, and so on.

A surprising amount of metadata can be captured automatically, as we explored in Chapter 1. Cameras can capture their own parameters—everything from aperture setting to filter wheel selections or focus information and zoom angle. Modern cameras can capture latitude, longitude, and altitude information and metadata such as time or the camera operator's name and the camera model and serial number. They can then wrap this into file formats such as the Material eXchange Format (MXF), developed by the Society of Motion Picture and Television Engineers (SMPTE), and pass it on to the next stage in the process where more information from other systems can be added automatically. This works similarly for graphics devices, telecines, and film equipment. In the postproduction suite, most of the technical parameters can be captured automatically and on the fly and again wrapped into a file format—formats such as the Advanced

Authoring Format (AAF) are specifically designed for this post use and are compatible also with MXF.

In the business domain, financial and management metadata is already well catered for in business IT systems. Much of this information can be of a confidential nature (salaries, payment details, bank information, etc.) and is therefore unlikely to be wrapped into an audiovisual file. However, the audiovisual file can (and probably will) certainly contain metadata that points to a computer server or file folder where the metadata can be found and contact details or how to access it. The exception might be intellectual property–related metadata where licensing dates and terms or embargo information can be advantageously wrapped with the audiovisual material to which it relates.

But the biggest application area for automatic capture of metadata is as yet barely addressed. As technology matures and becomes ever less expensive and as the number of channels increases exponentially, the demand for more and more programming also increases—but the money available does not. The volume of programs made is higher than it ever has been, but the profit margins are smaller than they ever have been. Interestingly, this mirrors the equipment domain, where the volume of equipment sold is also higher than it ever has been, but the new technologies mean that the unit cost is much lower so that margins are squeezed here too. At the same time, there is growing competition between channels for viewers, so programs have to be increasingly attractive.

The combination of more channels and interactivity will explode the demand for annotative metadata and a richer production mix to satisfy consumer demand and maintain a channel's audience. In addition, anything that enhances the quantity and quality of metadata brings two important benefits. One is the improved navigation for consumer and program researcher alike with the additional benefits of improved speed and accuracy. The other advantage is improved semantic definition and recognition—both of which can be used to increase viewer share and hence revenues.

This combination represents a huge and largely unrecognized opportunity in program production for anyone with library science or knowledge management skills. Existing material is being seen as both an in-house research resource and as a source of material, both previously seen and unseen, which can be inexpensively repurposed and used in new programs. If these opportunities are to be exploited to best advantage, then knowledge of the resource base needs to be professionally managed by a librarian or knowledge manager so that it can be fully exploited.

Technology that is currently in its embryonic stage promises the possibility of automatically capturing metadata that previously has had to be documented laboriously by hand, if at all—such tasks as transcribing speech to text; deriving keywords from spoken language; recognizing and identifying music, voices, and faces; identifying shot in and out points; capturing camera angles (note the implications for interactivity); recording audience reactions and emotions; recording the time key events happen; logging key sounds and pictures (such as a crowd roar, sudden movement); and capturing text in the picture (from a scoreboard or name caption). In the past it simply was not possible to capture the majority of these types of metadata due to limitations of time and effort, particularly for the live production of big sporting events such as the Olympic Games where many events happen in parallel and sometimes in different time zones. If many of these functions can be achieved automatically, even at only an 80 percent rate of capture, enormous potential is opened up as the library scientist or knowledge manager is freed from mundane and tedious tasks. A human will still need to provide context to footage to help retrieval—something a machine cannot do. For example, the digital asset management system can be programmed to recognize Richard Nixon's face. A visual recognition search for footage of "Richard Nixon" could possibly retrieve footage of antiwar demonstrators wearing Nixon masks. A cataloger will need to add descriptive information to the clip so it will be indexed appropriately with the correct context.

Many of these automatic metadata-generation technologies are, as previously mentioned, already in the embryonic stage, and although they are not yet fully functional, they soon will be. For example, speech recognition is already becoming commonplace, with limited lexicons for a large number of voices or a considerable range of vocabulary for a single voice.

Who Owns the Metadata?

If many people contribute to the creation of metadata, then who "owns" it? With metadata, ownership can have several meanings: who is authorized to enforce, edit, and approve the metadata (workflow ownership); who owns the intellectual content or rights (can metadata even be copyrighted? Some organizations think so); and who has ultimate responsibility if the metadata is wrong, resulting in the incorrect programs being aired or the wrong clips sold (business ownership)—not to mention who goes to prison if the metadata turns out to be scandalous or libelous.

Workflow Ownership

In the metadata creation workflow, it is most efficient to have one person with authority to instruct and give final approval of the metadata. Ideally, this would be a person with a library science or information management background. It is unusual in the United States, although less so in Europe, to find broadcast companies (other than news divisions) with a distinct cataloging department, and even then, the catalogers are recording content data after they have received tapes or footage rather than inputting data at the beginning of the production stream.

In the cases where metadata is solely input by trained catalogers following specific rules outlined by their department, ownership of the metadata is still not clear as there might be contention between a contracted company doing cataloging work and the production organization that owns the program rights.

However, most of the world's broadcasters do not have distinct cataloging departments. When they do, metadata creation occurs organically, following workflow as outlined in Chapter 2. Even if dispersed metadata creation is the practice, there should still be one person responsible for managing the metadata creation. This person would teach interdepartmental staff how to create their portion of the metadata. The metadata manager would establish rules and controlled vocabularies as well as check the data. But the metadata manager must have the authority to enforce the rules. All the training and handbooks in the world will not help to create meaningful metadata if the contributing staff have the attitude of "You're not my boss! You can't tell me what to do!" Administration has to make it clear that the metadata manager has authority to enforce workflow procedures. Otherwise, personality conflicts and turf wars will discourage staff members from taking their metadata responsibilities seriously or from doing the work well at all, with resultant workflow confusion, system failures, loss of material, and overflowing storage devices—which will prove to be full of the "lost" material.

Legal Information and Metadata Content Ownership

Legal information and metadata can operate at two levels: one where legal information is contained in the metadata, and one where the legal department "owns" the metadata. The metadata should contain information about the program's creation and any use restrictions. A more abstract relationship is the notion of who actually owns the copyright to the metadata and can it be legally "owned" in the first place?

Legal Information

As outlined in Chapter 2, legal information must appear in the metadata at various stages in the workflow. During the preproduction stage, it can include information such as the dates contracts with talent or locations were secured, and limited information as to the terms of the contracts. This information might not be useful during the postproduction stage, so preproduction legal metadata often finds itself included in a table linked to the primary record for the program.

Intellectual property rights must also be tracked in the metadata. Who owns the rights to the script? The music? The clips purchased? What is the duration of the license? Can the music be used for DVD release or only for broadcast? All of this information must be tracked, and it can best be input by the legal department since the actual contracts and files are held there.

Legal information must be "owned" by the legal department. There is a good business reason to limit access to legal data, where few staff can read it and even fewer have authority to edit this data. Wrong legal information can result in lawsuits against the company. Using an image of the talent's face for a billboard advertisement when this kind of exposure was not allowed in the person's contract can result in not just a lawsuit, but also wasted staff time and production costs—not to mention embarrassment for the company.

The legal department should work closely with and trust the metadata manager. While the legal department might "own" its data, the metadata manager should check it for misspellings and poor use of controlled vocabularies.

Legal Ownership of the Metadata

It should be obvious that the business that owns the programs described by the metadata owns the metadata it creates as well. There are a few examples where this might not be the case, although it would be difficult to find cases where lawsuits were brought for metadata copyright infringement. One example of a third party "owning" metadata for programs created by content creators is cataloging records created by university libraries or archives. These public institutions can acquire broadcasting materials and expend much time cataloging them and providing detailed descriptions and summaries.[1] Nevertheless, the fact that these records are created in educational institutions or with government funds (in the case of the American Film Institute catalogs) implies that their cataloging records are in the public domain, free for anyone to use in another context.

Another example is metadata created for the consumer. A broadcaster's website can contain detailed information about its programs; all that data is created by the broadcaster. Is data created for TV-Anytime or video on demand owned by the broadcaster or the VOD distributor? This is a difficult question to fully answer. Certainly some organizations would have a strong opinion on who owned thumbnail pictures, browse video, or transcribed speech—why not all the other metadata?

Business Ownership

Much of the liability for incorrect data can be blamed on the difficulty in authenticating the metadata. How can it be guaranteed that the metadata is correct when so much of it has been created by humans who are fallible? How can a broadcast operation be certain that the digital file it is about to deliver to millions of viewers

---

[1] For examples of full cataloging records that can be used as reference sources, see records created by the University of California, Los Angeles Film and Television Archive; the University of Georgia (Peabody Awards Collection records); and the American Film Institute Catalog.

is the correct one? Even if the title is correct in the metadata, is it the correct version? Moving toward capturing automatic data to avoid human error is possible in news gathering, where a camera that can embed UMID (Unique Material Identifier) information in digital files can track the date, production organization, and geographic location of the capture. This information will follow the digital file—including excerpts—as the file is incorporated into other programs. While this sounds like a good means to authenticate footage and ownership, the technology has not quite caught up to the ideal just yet. If the digital file is copied through another machine that captures UMID information, it will assign the new UMID information to the digital file, wiping out the original data and destroying the possibility for automatic authentication, although if SMPTE recommended practices are followed, it will contain an audit trail right back to the original camera material. Until technology develops to the degree that authentication of digital files is guaranteed, humans will remain the primary metadata creators, caretakers, and authenticators.

Practicalities and Opportunities of Desktop Production in the New Workflows

Audiovisual (AV) media files are, by their very nature, large, with video files being exceedingly large—even if they are compressed into professional recording formats. This already considerable size will increase as production changes to higher definitions and will potentially do so again when production companies start working with resolution independent techniques (as are already found in regular office software, which explains why when composing PowerPoint presentations it is not necessary to know about the display on which they will eventually be shown) since this implies a production format with sufficient information to extract all other formats from it.

In practical terms, it will not be realistic to cost-effectively distribute such native AV files to office desktops in the near future, so members of the production crew will not be able to access them directly from their office desks. Instead, they must work with a version of the content that represents it completely by substituting a lower resolution proxy of the original video along with the metadata accompanying the original, such as library descriptions, time-code, edit decision lists (EDLs), frame numbers, color correction data, negative conform lists, and so on. This proxy can itself be accurately regarded as metadata because of its descriptive nature and can vary from low-definition thumbnails to focus-quality moving images that are frame accurate with the original and, as already mentioned, are often loosely referred to as "browse video."

Making such a proxy is not as trivial a task as it might first appear. It has to be done in such a way that additional information is reliably coupled to it frame by frame and so that operations carried out on the proxy are accurately reflected in the final, full-resolution result without additional mouse clicks or keyboard strokes necessitated by virtue of working with the proxy. The final result must also accurately contain all the relevant metadata. Deciding what "relevant data" refers to is also a nontrivial task, the technology for which, at the time of this writing, has not been fully developed other than for technical metadata. However, this process of collecting metadata during the program creation process will become gradually more important, and eventually metadata collecting mechanisms will overlay the whole production process as a transparent system layer.

In every case, the unambiguous indexing of the material, whether collected on the fly in production (ideal) or later added by hand annotation, will be very important since it will be crucial when searching for and retrieving content, whether computer aided or not. The day when a computer system can find the image you have in mind without your exactly describing it with computer algorithms is still a long way off.

Key in this new world is good management of knowledge. This implies that not only must the interaction between human and machine be intuitive and effective, but that networking at a human level between members of a production or supporting team must be at least as effective as the networking between computers. In its most basic form, this implies that fundamental human needs are well taken care of—for instance, a relaxed meeting place around the coffee machine may be really crucial. Seriously though, it can in practice be a real problem to get everyone to the same level of skills or understanding. The creative computer nerd somewhere in the corner may well be essential, but this person could equally well have ideas and interests so far removed from creative program makers in the same team as to be intensely irritating to them. Sharing tacit knowledge, expertise, and skills across different disciplines, interests, and personalities is not a natural ability in most people but will be important to the end game, and this will be a real challenge for the management of such a production environment.

The management of rights is not a new problem, but its implications in the digital domain are only just becoming apparent. Consumers not only require access to the content they want, but they require it *now* and they require it unencumbered— they are no longer prepared to pay for 13 tracks of a CD just to get the one track they like. This implies a completely new methodology in exploitation if people are to be persuaded that something is worth paying for and represents good value for the money. Further, the introduction of digital systems that interoperate seamlessly has implications for rights management everywhere in program production—for example, in a facilities company working for many clients and on several productions simultaneously using the same digital system. In this kind of organization it will be crucial to give clients confidence that nobody outside their own production crew can access their content. Any chance of leaking the content must be minimized to zero.

71

Where Can Metadata Leak Away?

With paper information systems and discrete physical cassettes for the audiovisual material, things did get lost from time to time. This was inconvenient but could usually be solved by a good search around the production office, in drawers, in filing cabinets, and on shelves. Because there was a physical piece of paper, cassette, or another object and some idea of where it was last seen, time and effort put into turning the office upside down usually paid off. The weak points in the system were at the interfaces between workflow processes, where the picture and sound were handed on, but the accompanying notes and other information rarely were (the sole exception being time-code, because it was usually recorded onto the same physical medium as the pictures and sound).

Digital systems are very different. To a computer system, all data look the same—documents, spreadsheets, video and audio files are all just binary data and can be handled as such. The downside is that all such data are invisible, intangible, and cannot be seen, touched, or picked up. In a big system with many computers and file servers, it may not even be clear exactly where your data are located—on the file server down the corridor or the one across the Atlantic? All data are the same—just a sequence of ones and zeros. If something gets lost in a computer system, it stays lost—there is generally no way to find it.

Digital assets are defined as the combination of metadata and "essence" (e.g., content in the digital file) plus the right to use it. One without the other does not constitute an asset; the separated components are then "orphans." In a way, this cartesian separation is similar to the separate lives of analog media and its corresponding metadata: a videotape of a program can sit on the shelf, while its metadata record exists as a card in a file. Storing the components separately—whether they are analog or digital—makes linking them carefully all the more crucial.

So managing the data and metadata becomes paramount, as even a simple spelling mistake can render days of work untraceable. The undisciplined use of naming conventions as well as the use of slang terms, abbreviations, and shortcuts are fatal in this domain. Laziness in naming is a real enemy and can quickly lead to chaos—names such as "shot1," "Solent Today Friday," "billv1," and the like are particularly fatal. Learning the discipline of naming conventions is a must, but it comes very hard to people who are used to focusing in a different way. Increasingly, intelligent software may alleviate some of the worst sensitivity to spelling errors and similar problems, but it is unlikely ever to be able to properly untangle the context and conceptual aspects of what "shot1" really is.

In the archive, it is possible for information to leak away by simply being deleted. This is an old problem, what to keep and what to delete, and much comes down to the skill of the archivist. Archivists have training in appraisal and records management, so they can advise the content creators and owners about what should be kept and what can be discarded. Not every bit of metadata needs to be saved in all situations. However, once metadata is deleted, it is lost forever, and although it can to some extent be re-created, this will always be expensive and a poor substitute at best for the original.

Even if the pictures and sound are deleted, the metadata associated with them can still be invaluable as a source of information and knowledge in later research: a lot of metadata can be stored in a very small space and at little cost in a modern computer system. The usefulness of "orphan" metadata in research is especially appreciated in the educational community, where information on a program's production can be researched in a public catalog for scholarly articles, books, program notes, and so on.

Authenticity in Metadata

During the creation and implementation of a production's technical infrastructure, important decisions have to be made: What kinds of metadata need to be captured and stored? How can it be consulted and by whom? Does metadata need to be embedded into the audiovisual file or stream? Should the metadata just be solidly connected to it technically, or can it be held in a completely separate database? Should it be accessible from outside the department using intranet access, and should this facility be extended over the Internet to those outside the organization? If the metadata will be stored both with the audiovisual material and in a separate database as well, how can the two be kept synchronized? None of these is a trivial task, and all are expensive to implement. They need to be justified in terms of commercial return on the financial investment in the system.

When addressing the question of whether to keep metadata in the file itself as well as in a separate database, it needs to be clear which record is the master or authenticated data and who is entitled to change it or add to it. Should the mirror always be synchronized after any change in the master or vice versa? When the master metadata is in a separate database and the mirror is in the file, synchronization after each change will be costly and time consuming as the file will have to be retrieved, transferred to a server or workstation, opened, rewritten, closed, and rearchived. Similarly, if the master database is in the stored content, any modification will have this loading and unloading problem and therefore will be equally costly. Solutions to this problem will probably be found in in-between solutions where the master metadata is in a database, separate from the actual content, and a tracking system is employed to log the use of stored content and changes to it or to its metadata. Then, every time a piece of material is retrieved and loaded to a server for examination or for further use, that opportunity can be used to update and synchronize the mirror kept in the file with the master metadata—in many cases this could even be carried out at the frame level. This kind of infrastructure obviously needs both a sophisticated information system alongside the content database and the skills necessary to understand broadcast

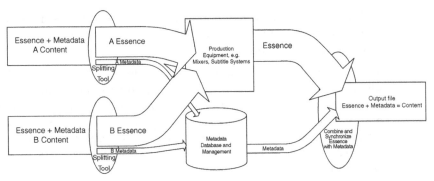

Figure 4.1.

production requirements, the technology of material-containing file formats, and the technology of the IT infrastructure.

As we saw in Chapter 1, when metadata is embedded into the audiovisual material or contained in the file, problems of a similar kind occur if the material needs further processing—for example, if it is to undergo reworking such as mixing, editing, or adding a logo for transmission (Figure 4.1). What happens to the output stream during a dissolve between metadata-containing video streams? What metadata needs to be carried through to the output stream—in the case of a transmission area, should it be all of the input metadata or just some of it for onward transmission to viewers? It is likely therefore that the content and the metadata will be split with the metadata being put aside into a temporary database cache. This has the double advantage of minimizing the accidental loss of any metadata and allowing the metadata to be easily worked on to create the new program metadata or version of the program metadata. The drawback is that putting the metadata back into place in the audiovisual file or stream automatically is a complex IT operation. Synchronization mechanisms have yet to be invented to do this, but commercial justification for this kind of relatively costly process might be found in the use of the material. If the program content is serving a potentially large market, the members of this market should know (indeed, will want to know) in advance what programming they will get from that provider. If some of the more advanced metadata really adds value to that content, consumers will probably be prepared to pay extra for it. This means that the transmission system, the playout system, and the digital encoding systems should be capable of dealing with this advanced and charged-for metadata and providing it in a format that an application can understand and use interactively.

Mapping Metadata to Different Systems

At every stage in the program-making workflow there are different processes involved and different criteria applied. For example, the processes and criteria in the planning stage have, on the surface, little in common with the processes and criteria in the edit suite or the archive. Traditionally, this has meant that each stage has had its own way of doing things and used its own terminology and system. The result has been that terms and words in common use throughout the industry have come to mean different things in different parts of the workflow. Metadata is, unfortunately, no exception. Until now, interfacing between these differing areas was carried out by human effort, and any ambiguity as metadata was moved from one process to the next in the workflow was addressed by the people involved, who simply sorted it out between themselves. Now that the opportunity exists to connect one digital process to another, any ambiguity at the interface will cause serious problems and, in the case of technical metadata, probably a system failure. For example, in an XML schema, each metadata element will be defined in a strict context defined by that schema. It is likely that different schemas will be used on either side of an interface, so great care is needed to pass not only the metadata element but also its context. Reusing a metadata element in this way is unlikely to be trivial in system terms. Clearly, having one overarching metadata scheme for a whole organization would minimize problems within that organization. Achieving this goal will not be a trivial task and will not address interoperability issues between organizations—hence the future need for agreed international standards.

5 Identifiers and Identification

There is an old and perceptive saying—"A little knowledge is a dangerous thing," and this cannot be more true than in the case of identifiers.

Everywhere in broadcasting, words like "ISAN," "UMID," "AUID," "MAC address," "UUID," and "Instance Number" are bandied around. They are knowledgeable-sounding acronyms beloved by some who have no understanding of what they identify, what their intended use is, or even what the letters stand for. This can be dangerously misleading, and the consequences will not begin to show up until a system is commissioned and put to work (or more likely, until it fails to work).

When considering identifiers, it is important to be clear at every stage exactly what is being identified—for example, a work (such as musical composition), something physical (such as a videotape cassette), a nebulous technical detail (such as a sequence of video frames), or an administrative detail (such as a costing code). Each aspect must be identified separately because trying to use an identifier for a purpose for which it was not intended will always cause confusion in later processes.

The following scenario demonstrates the way in which identifiers relate to each other. The "object record" concept described in Chapter 3 helps provide a metadata structure for this example.

> In order for an audience to enjoy a work, it must be performed and each performance will be separate and unique (it will have its own time and place). If each performance is recorded in stereo for television using two recorders (a main and a backup), there will be several recordings of the same work (one from each performance) and two instances of each recording. In intellectual terms, both instances are the same; but in physical terms,

they are each unique and each include both one picture and two sound essences. In this case the work, each performance, each recording, each instance, and the picture and sound material within each instance will be separately identified.

In the digital domain, unambiguous and unique identification is absolutely paramount because anything stored in a computer system is both invisible and intangible. If any of the relationships in the preceding example are corrupted or wrong, the system will fail and is likely to fail catastrophically.

First, one must become familiar with some of the terminology commonly used with broadcasting technology. Note that the following list is not exhaustive, and different bodies and organizations use different terms and meanings (for instance, the performing rights community often talks about *manifestation* when referring to the recording of a performance onto physical media):

Identifier. A symbol that serves to identify, indicate, or name.

Work. A completed artistic creation, produced or accomplished through the effort, activity, or agency of a person or group.

Version. A particular form or variation of an earlier or original work.

Essence. Any data or signal necessary to represent any single type of visual, aural, or other sensory experience.

Material. Any one or any combination of picture essences, sound essences, and other essences.

Label. An identifier once it has been bound to its material.

Instance. A specific and unique occurrence of material, metadata, or content.

Content. Material and any associated metadata.

Metadata. That data that convey information about material—for example, information about identification, essence decoding, time lines, intellectual property, business operations.

Namespace. A uniquely identified collection of names intended for identification of metadata contained in logical structures. For example, eXtensible Mark-up Language (XML) namespaces, which are uniquely identified by an Internet Engineering Task Force Uniform Resource Identifier (URI).

Unique identifiers fall into several categories:

- Identifiers registered by an international registration authority (e.g., an International Standard Book Number [ISBN]) and guaranteed to be unique internationally. Creating each identifier always costs money.
- Identifiers registered by a local registration authority (e.g., a broadcaster's program number) and guaranteed to be unique within a given organization. This organization may in turn be uniquely registered internationally, potentially making such identifiers internationally unique for a single payment.
- Unregistered identifiers, which are generated in such a way as to guarantee their uniqueness globally (e.g., an Internet engineering task force universally unique identifier [UUID] or a Society of Motion Picture and Television

Engineers [SMPTE] unique material identifier [UMID]). These are normally free.

Given a registered identifier, it is a relatively trivial task to trace back through the register and find out when it was issued, what for, and to whom. With unregistered identifiers, this is clearly far from trivial, if possible at all. For example, given only an ISBN of "0-14-044107-7," most people would know it identifies a book; a bookshop can quickly identify both it and the publisher and order a copy. Given only a UUID of "6fdf4290-ae8b-11d9-9669-0800200c9a66" there is little chance of finding out what it identifies, though it is possible to extract some detail such as the time it was created.

The good news is that unregistered unique identifiers are nearly all low-level identifiers, generated and used by the inner workings of a digital system for tracking the data it needs. A user is unaware of them. Two examples are the UUID used within desktop PCs or the UMID used within media systems for their own inner workings. Most people quite happily use their home or office PCs without worrying about UUIDs, and the same is true for UMIDs when capturing or editing pictures or sound. It is important to appreciate that these sorts of identifiers are necessary for internal technical processing within a system and are not there to identify the content or intellectual property contained within it—using them for that will confuse systems and will cause system failure.

Some identifiers can preexist content or be allocated later; others cannot—for example, the program number may preexist content, whereas the UMID cannot because none will be generated until picture or sound are first captured, and a decision to purchase an International Standard Audiovisual Number (ISAN) may be made after a program is completed and it has been decided that the cost is justified.

Apart from the possible cost of registered identifiers, the big advantage of unregistered identifiers is the speed at which they can independently be made available within a device—in a modern electronic system, usually within a space of a few microseconds. Although locally registered numbers can be made available almost as fast, this requires the overhead of some form of connection to a central point.

Unique identifiers frequently contain several pieces of metadata, often but not always delineated by commas, hyphens, or spaces. This can make them difficult to deal with within a computer system where a simple dumb and meaningless number is preferable, provided it is unique. Although such an identifier is always displayed fully in a field, it may beneficially be stored as its separate parts.

Registered Identifiers

International Registration Authorities

There are literally hundreds, if not thousands, of bodies acting as registration authorities. Some of these operate under the auspices of the International

Standards Organisation (for example, the Society of Motion Picture and Television Engineers [SMPTE]), while many do not (for example, the Internet Assigned Number Authority [IANA] who allocates domain names etc.). Frequently the actual issuing of identifiers is subcontracted to other agencies (as, for example, by the International Standard Audiovisual Number [ISAN] International Agency). Many are private companies using identifiers purely for their own internal use.

The following table attempts to list those registration organizations most relevant to broadcasting along with some of their typical identifiers. This list is not exhaustive, however, and does not include registered country codes, languages, currency, and other details because these are not identifiers in the sense of this document.

Organization	Typical Relevant Identifiers	Relevance	Registered
International Standards Organisation (ISO) *www.iso.org*	ISO Audio-Visual Number (ISAN) ISO Version identifier for audiovisual works (V-ISAN) ISO Musical Work Code (ISWC) ISO Recording Code (ISRC) ISO Textual Work Code (ISTC) and many others	Program production	Internationally
Society of Motion Picture and Television Engineers Registration Authority *www.smpte-ra.org*	Metadata Registry Key Universal Label	Program production	Organizationally under ISO
International DOI Foundation *www.doi.org*	Digital Object Identifier (DOI)	Program production and production to consumer	Internationally
Institution of Electrical & Electronic Engineers (IEEE) *www.ieee.org*	Device Identifier (Network Node Identifier) (commonly also called the MAC address)	Program production	Internationally
European Broadcasting Union *www.ebu.ch*	Broadcasting Organisation Facility Code Country and Network Identifiers (CNI)	Program production	Organizationally
Internet Engineering Task Force (IETF) *www.ietf.org*	Uniform Resource Identifiers (URI)	Program production	Internationally

Organization	Typical Relevant Identifiers	Relevance	Registered
Digital Video Broadcasting (DVB) *www.dvb.org*	System Information Identifiers (SI IDs) Multimedia Home Platform Application IDs	Production to consumer	Internationally
Advanced Television Systems Committee (ATSC) *www.atsc.org*	System Information Identifiers (SI IDs) Packet Identifiers (PID) Unique Program Identifier (UPI)	Production to consumer	Internationally
Internet Assigned Numbers Authority (IANA) *www.iana.org*	Internet domain names I.P. addresses port numbers and so on	Production to consumer	Internationally
Content ID Forum *www.cidf.org*	Content ID (cIDF)	Production to consumer	Organizationally
TV-Anytime Forum *www.tv-anytime.org*	Content Reference ID (CRID)	Production to consumer	Resolves elsewhere
Corporation for National Research Initiatives (CNRI) *www.cnri.reston.va.us*	CNRI Handle	Production to consumer	Resolves elsewhere
ITV Association	Unique Program Number (UPN)	Textual records	Organizationally
International Federation of Library Associations and Institutions *www.ifla.org*	Bibliographic Descriptor (ISBC)	Textual records	Organizationally
ANSI/NISO *www.ansi.org*	Book Item and Component Identifier (BICI) Serial Item and Contribution Identifier (SICI)	Textual records	Internationally
American Chemical Society *www.acs.org*	Publisher Item Identifier (PII)	Textual records	Organizationally
American Association of Advertising Agencies *www.aaaa.org*	Commercial Identifier (ISCI)	Textual records	Organizationally
European Telecommunications Standards Institute *www.etsi.org*	Object Identifiers (Usually delegated to IANA [see above]) Teletext Technical Identifiers	Textual records	Internationally

Organizations classed as having program production relevance and their areas of application are outlined next. Those organizations classed in the preceding table as having production-to-consumer relevance are generally intimately concerned with broadcasting but concentrate on the business-to-consumer part of the chain. It is therefore important to know they exist and have an interest, but in general their work does not cover program production or postproduction.

Identifiers with Program Production Relevance

International Standards Organisation

ISO is a network of the national standards institutes of 148 countries, on the basis of one member per country, with a central secretariat in Geneva, Switzerland, that coordinates the system. The standardization process through ISO is of necessity slow, but the resultant standards are well respected and generally well adhered to. In the broadcasting world, standards for identifiers have generally related to the business-to-consumer-domain and tend to be in the context of intellectual property management and e-trading.

Currently, the most relevant Standard is the ISAN which identifies all types of audiovisual works and their relevant versions. Registrations and therefore ISAN allocation are done via Registration Agencies which lately have been appointed in Europe, USA and Australia. ISANs are purchased from one of the ISAN agencies for a relatively small one-off charge. An ISAN permanently identifies an audiovisual work and its versions at every point in its lifecycle from conception through production and distribution to consumption. The ISAN central repository contains a set of specific descriptive metadata about the works, episodes and versions of works.

Society of Motion Picture and Television Engineers Registration Authority (SMPTE-RA)

This is the registration authority of the SMPTE, and it operates as a separately incorporated company from its parent organization. It is unusual in that some registrations are charged for and some not, depending on the application. It is the custodian of the SMPTE Metadata Registries, though currently only the SMPTE Metadata Dictionary (or Register of Metadata Elements) and the Labels Registry are published on the website, with the Groups, Controlled Vocabularies (or Enumerations) and Datatypes Registries due during 2005 and 2006. The SMPTE registration at the top level of the registries is unique under ISO, so each entry in turn is internationally unique. Each metadata registry can also serve as a root for a namespace (see the terminology listed earlier). Entries in the registers are free if the entry is subjected to international due process scrutiny; otherwise there is a charge.

International Digital Object Identifier (DOI) Foundation

This not-for-profit membership organization has spun out of the rights and intellectual property community and is a system for identifying content objects in the digital environment. The DOI has recently been appointed as the registration authority of the MPEG21 Rights Data Dictionary. DOIs (recently also called digital item identifiers, DII) can be used to identify many things such as an abstract work (which can often only be perceived indirectly—for example by being performed) or a person (who is more than simply a set of data).

Digital object identifiers are names assigned to any entity for use on digital networks. The DOI system is claimed to provide a framework for supplying persistent identification, managing intellectual content and metadata, linking customers with content suppliers, facilitating electronic commerce, and enabling automated management of media. The DOI is a key component of the CNRI handle (discussed later). DIIs are purchased from the foundation and there is a charge for each one issued.

Institution of Electrical & Electronic Engineers (IEEE)

The IEEE is probably the senior organization in the United States dealing with things electrical. It was formed in the last half of the 19th century, in the days of the telegraph and the introduction of electricity into the home.

These days it has sections devoted to modern computing and electronics and issues both standards and registers. One of its most important standards is that of numbering for network devices—all network devices, including those used in broadcasting, have a device identifier with a unique number, which is often called the medium access control (MAC) address. This number, in conjunction with time, forms the basis for nearly all unregistered unique identifiers including UUIDs and UMIDs, and its importance in this respect cannot be overstressed. Manufacturers purchase blocks of numbers for their manufacturing of devices, but it is unlikely that a broadcaster would purchase any directly—rather, a broadcasting company would purchase a device along with its number (for example, a network card in a desktop PC). Modern digital devices in use in broadcasting all have networking capability (cameras, servers, graphics workstations, etc.), so they all have a network device with a unique MAC address.

It cannot be overstated that the MAC address is a key identifier in today's digital technology. Although it is a very low level identifier, it is registered and every network node, card, or access point in use in any computer anywhere in the world will have its own unique MAC address. If your own computer has two network ports, it will have two MAC addresses. Normally, the MAC is invisible to the user—but if you have a networking problem, the MAC address is one of the first things an information technology (IT) person will look for. It will be recorded both electronically within the PC and written on the labels on the PC, PC card, or wireless device. It is written, in hexadecimal notation, like this: 00C049BC96EC or 00.C0.49.BC.96.EC. Do not underestimate this identifier.

European Broadcasting Union (EBU)

The EBU has member broadcasters throughout Europe, but it is not a recognized formal standardization body. It administers a large and complex network for exchanging program material between members. However, it does issue some of its own identifiers, such as the Broadcasting Organisation Facility Codes, used in some Broadcast Wave Format audio files, Tape Numbering, and the Country and Network Identifiers used for Teletext in conjunction with ETSI.

Internet Engineering Task Force (IETF)

This is the major standards-setting body for the Internet and is an open international community of network designers, operators, vendors, and researchers concerned with the evolution of the Internet architecture and the smooth operation of the Internet.

It delegates registration matters to IANA but controls standards such as the uniform resource identifier (URI), which is used to track and uniquely identify Internet resources. The URI is becoming increasingly important as eXtensible Markup Language (XML) develops. URIs are not registered but behave in a similar way to Internet addresses (which are registered and for which a registration fee is payable).

Summary: Registered Identifiers

Most unique identifiers in current use in program production and postproduction are either related to intellectual property and issued by a central registration authority or are low-level identifiers related to the innermost workings of digital systems and invisible to the normal user.

It is possible to purchase a block of unique identifiers from ISO, the SMPTE, or the DOI. Both the ISO and the DOI are focusing on rights issues. The SMPTE tends to be more technical and production oriented. The block size that is allocated under the SMPTE's "Organizationally Registered for Private Use" in each register is enormous and gives total freedom for an organization to "do its own thing" while still guaranteeing no clashes of identifiers.

Unregistered Identifiers

There are, by definition, *no* registration authorities for unregistered identifiers. But there are controlling standards for generating these identifiers:

- Standards from an international standards-making body such as the Internet Engineering Task Force or the Society of Motion Picture and Television Engineers

- Proprietary standards written by a manufacturer purely for use within the manufacturer's own devices, with no guarantee they are unique outside of that manufacturer's products

Proprietary standards are not further considered in this book.

In general, unregistered identifiers are numbers generated by following one of three conventions:

- Using a random number algorithm
- Using a registered identifier in conjunction with time
- Using a combination of the two

Two examples of unregistered identifiers used in broadcasting are the UMID and UUID, both of which by default use the IEEE device identifier (i.e., a MAC address) as the registered identifier. Each has its own place and its own use, and both are generated by the third method noted in the preceding list—that is, a combination of a registered identifier (such as a MAC address), time, and a random number (usually included for additional security), though the SMPTE UMID can also use a UUID or other appropriate 16-byte-long identifier as its basic core. Each can, optionally, be masked to prevent reverse engineering of a given UMID or UUID to determine the time it was created or the MAC address used in its creation.

Unique Material Identifier (UMID)

The basic UMID is a specialist identifier used in digital audiovisual systems and is a low-level system component used when instantiating pictures and sound as essence. Its purpose is to enable the linking of essence to its associated metadata so that all the components needed to enable a file (or stream) to be manipulated or viewed can be tracked and made available in the correct relationship. A basic UMID can optionally have an extension consisting of a metadata pack with frame count, location information, and an identifier for the person or company operating the capturing device (camera, audio recorder, etc.). This means each individual frame of captured video (or audio) can be separately identified, as can the latitude and longitude of the capturing device and the person or company who recorded it. Each of these extension fields is optional.

A new UMID is generated for each essence being captured by a device at the point in time when capturing begins—in the case of a camcorder, at the instant when the "record" button is pressed—and the same basic UMIDs apply until capturing stops. This means that in the case of a discontinuous recording to a hard disk, one or more streams of UMIDs will be generated—one stream for each essence type being captured, each stream containing UMIDs generated at each recording start time.

The UMID is, in general, specific to the particular instantiation—in other words, in the case of a recording, the specific segments in a specific track on a specific hard disk or optical disk or linear tape or whatever recording medium is being used. Equally, it will apply to a specific essence stream in the case of a live broadcast that is not being recorded. If essence is copied, the copy will have a new unique UMID. The exception to this rule is the case of a closed system, which is well managed if (and it is a big *if*) two instantiations can be guaranteed to be logically identical, in which case they may have the same UMID; however, this is a special case and will not be further considered here. If two sequences of essence are edited together, the newly created essence resulting from the edit will have its own unique UMID, and it should have an audit trail back to the UMIDs from which it was created.

A UMID is generated according to an SMPTE standard—SMPTE330M—and can, if generated using the appropriate method, be guaranteed to be unique for at least the next 1,200 years or so. It was first standardized in 2000, and the standard was updated in 2003 in a way that ensured backwards compatibility. The following is an extract from the scope of the standard:

The UMID is a unique identifier for audiovisual material which is locally created and globally unique. It differs from many unique identifiers in that the number does not depend wholly upon a pre-registration process, but can be generated automatically at the point of material origination without reference to a central resource.

The UMID provides a method of identification for instances of audiovisual material and thus enables the material to be linked with its associated metadata. The UMID itself is neither intended for the identification of copyright nor the ownership of rights. Nor, for example, does it identify program content or Works.

The UMID consists of an ordered group of components each providing a key aspect to the identification of the audiovisual material, be it picture, sound or data. A key property of a UMID generated in accordance with this standard is that it is possible to use the resulting UMID simply as a globally unique dumb number.

Note the very clear warning in the scope: "The UMID itself is neither intended for the identification of copyright nor the ownership of rights. Nor, for example, does it identify program content or Works." There is common misunderstanding and misinformation about the UMID in that respect; be very clear, however, that the UMID is intended to be a low-level identifier used for identifying a particular instantiation of specific essence, no more and no less.

Universal Unique Identifier (UUID)

The defining standard for creating a UUID, also known as a globally unique identifier (or GUID), is ISO/IEC 11578, annex A. This standard derived from an IETF original (which in many ways is more user-friendly than the ISO standard) in about 1998.

If generated according to one of the methods in the ISO standard, a UUID is either guaranteed to be different from all other UUIDs generated until 3400 A.D. or extremely likely to be different (depending on the generating option chosen). The UUID is generated in a very similar way to the UMID, using the IEEE device identifier (MAC address) and time. There are many options and alternatives for how the time stamp is generated, how the random numbers are generated, and so on.

UUIDs are widely used for multiple purposes in IT systems, for everything from tracking file components with an extremely short lifetime to reliably identifying persistent digital objects across an IT network. UUIDs are also used to track generations as data are modified and hence are used in audit trails to track parent-child relationships. They are therefore used in everything from simple desktop PC applications such as spreadsheets or word processing to complex audio-visual systems where they are used to track the nonessence data within a system.

As with the UMID, UUIDs are specific to a particular instantiation of data—if the same data appears more than once in a system, or appears in multiple independent or networked systems, each occurrence will have a unique UUID. As with the UMID, the UUID does not identify copyright, ownership rights, program content, or works.

Summary: Unregistered Identifiers

Unregistered identifiers are very low level internal identifiers that the system user does not normally see. However, there is much misunderstanding about what they identify and what they are for. In fact, it is worth being wary of any recommendation to use an unregistered identifier because such a recommendation is probably the result of a misunderstanding—for example, a recommendation to use a UMID to identify a work such as a program demonstrates this lack of understanding as to what the UMID is identifying. Recordings of identical picture material recorded simultaneously on two identical recorders will have *different* UMIDs. This useful property means that if you have identical recordings in two or more places within a digital system, you can tell which is which.

Identifiers with Production to Consumer Relevance

Digital Video Broadcasting Project (DVB)

This industry-led consortium is made up of more than 260 broadcasters, manufacturers, network operators, software developers, regulatory bodies, and others in more than 35 countries. The group develops standards for the delivery of digital television and data services. Services using DVB standards are available almost worldwide (including the United States for nonterrestrial applications). The DVB project allocates identifiers for its own internal technical use and also issues identifiers to other bodies likely to make use of DVB technology—for example, the Internet Engineering Task force or the ISO MPEG Committee.

Advanced Television Systems Committee (ATSC)

The Advanced Television Systems Committee is a nonprofit organization based in the United States that develops standards for digital television. Specifically, ATSC is working to coordinate television standards focusing on digital television, interactive systems, and broadband multimedia communications. Like DVB, it allocates identifiers for its own internal technical use and also issues identifiers to other bodies likely to make use of its technology.

Internet Assigned Numbers Authority (IANA)

This is a body set up by the Internet Engineering Task Force and World Wide Web Consortium to administer the identifiers used in Internet and Web applications. Their Registrations include domain names (such as smpte.org) and the Internet Protocol (IP) addresses used by the Internet.

Content ID Forum (cIDF)

This organization, supported by approximately 200 Japanese companies, is working to standardize a unique identifier for digital content in order to provide a copyright management framework for Internet use. This framework will utilize watermarking technology and Internet-like technology to resolve the identity of the rights holders. The system is capable of resolving Content down to a level of a particular feature in a single frame of video, but is currently administratively rather cumbersome.

TV-Anytime Forum (TVA)

This association of organizations is developing specifications to enable audiovisual and other services based on mass-market, high-volume digital storage in consumer platforms—simply referred to as local storage. One key component is the content reference identifier (CRID), which is designed to be the bridge between content-related descriptive metadata and corresponding content audiovisual data location (i.e., where the content is stored as a file on, for example, the Internet). Since program content may be stored (and duplicated) in multiple locations at the same time across the world, this is less trivial an operation that it at first sight appears.

Corporation for National Research Initiatives (CNRI)

CNRI is a not-for-profit organization formed to foster research and development for the National Information Infrastructure of the United States. Among CNRI's major goals is a program of research into infrastructural technologies and services that will unlock the potential of information and knowledge along with technology itself. The CNRI handle operates much like the TV-Anytime CRID, but it is less focused on audiovisual data and more on administrative and business data, such as rights. The CNRI handle makes extensive use of the DOI (discussed earlier).

This chapter has presented a short summary of some of the identifiers that are currently used in broadcasting systems. There are literally thousands of identifiers in use in the industry, and it is worth repeating that the old rule of "horses for courses" applies, because trying to use an identifier for a purpose for which it was not intended will *always* cause confusion in later processes.

6 Metadata for the Consumer

New innovations offering a wider variety of communication network types to the consumer at home and a wide choice of bandwidths will change the use of content dramatically in the coming decade—already the penetration of technologies such as asymmetric digital subscriber line (ADSL) broadband and fiber to the home is changing things. The TV-Anytime business models inspired many application designers, and it is for that reason that this chapter takes the TV-Anytime specification as a guide. However, many other implementations follow these basic ideas.

Standards to communicate useful information from content providers to consumers are emerging rapidly, driven by major international projects such as Digital Video Broadcasting's Multimedia Home Platform (DVB-MHP) and TV-Anytime. Recently, these two projects effectively joined forces, with the DVB-MHP adoption of the TV-Anytime specification for implementing new services based on local storage in the consumer's home. At the same time, the USA Cablelabs group reached consensus with DVB-MHP resulting in the Cable Labs OpenCable Applications Platform (OCAP). This platform endorsed the DVB-MHP standard for global interoperability DVB-GEM (Global Executable MHP). Effectively DVB, OCAP, and TV-Anytime joined forces in 2003, and after two years of work the spec was ready for implementation in summertime 2005. While not all the features of TV-Anytime have been implemented, it is a good start and the process is not yet completed.

One of the major features of digital television implementation has been the electronic program guide (EPG), which is now becoming, in TV-Anytime's words, the electronic content guide (ECG) because it will not only point the consumer to complete television programs but to the whole overarching spectrum of digital content, including new consumer services as interactive additions to programs and other features are created to meet consumer demand.

An often unappreciated issue in the chain between the content provider and the consumer is that the standards for interactive content have frequently been developed by telecommunication operators and consumer electronics manufacturers. This has happened because many of the standards that are now being used were developed from telecommunications applications—for example, the MPEG video standards now in common use for television were developed from early videophone and video conferencing developments. As a result, program makers, librarians, and many others in the program-making chain were not involved during the development of these sometimes very complex technologies.

The set of standard features supported in practice by a consumer set-top box is based on the assumption that consumers want to have interface boxes at the lowest possible price, and this assumption has strongly influenced the functionality actually achieved in interactive systems. For example, in a specification such as TV-Anytime and its implementations in DVB-MHP, many useful features are "optional" and this has been interpreted by the consumer electronics industry as the option for it to leave a feature out and make the set-top box cheaper to develop and manufacture rather than an optional feature available to a content creator or available to the consumer to switch on or off. Sadly, in many examples this has led to set-top boxes that cannot do much more than basic decoding of the program without any of the additional functionality potentially offered by metadata-enabled digital systems. This has already led to a chicken-and-egg situation in the development and provision by content creators of more in-depth, more interactive, or more educational television. Although possible from a content creator's point of view, this kind of television programming is pointless until the consumer can make use of it—and the consumer will not invest in a more expensive set-top box until the content is available to be made use of. With interactive TV, it is important to draw the distinction between metadata and data downloaded for an interactive application, which may be additional data essence—that is, it is *not* metadata and it is not audio or video, but it *is* data that contribute to some form of human perception, for example a subtitle, vibration, or smell.

An example illustrates this point well. Nearly all set-top boxes manufactured up until now have only one built-in text font. The original specification offered the option for a limited number of downloadable fonts and newer versions of the specification extend this to most contemporary downloadable fonts. With only one standard font implemented in those boxes, all applications will look very much the same. The applications designers, therefore, do not have the freedom to "play" with available font types to get more effective communication with the participants of, for example, a game or TV lesson. Graphic designers working in the digital domain feel restricted by being limited to a single font. However, unless sufficient consumer electronic manufacturers choose to implement this option, graphic designers and interactive television (iTV) application developers will simply have no option to using the single available font. The metadata actually available for the use of fonts in TV production is at least as rich as that for electronic publications, but the dogma of "cost cutting at all costs" means that its use is simply not available to either consumer or program maker. Conversely, in other consumer industries we find a completely different attitude. Washing machine manufacturers, for example, have a range of washing machines in the shops, and consumers pick the machine with the functionality they want or need. In due course, market forces will no doubt lead to the same marketing philosophy for digital TV and set-top boxes.

Online: Yes or No?

Many of the new features in digital TV systems and devices need metadata that is not normally embedded in the traditional digital broadcast stream and so cannot be retrieved from the stream when needed. For this reason, many new types of devices are equipped with a computer network connection as well as the conventional TV, cable, satellite, or terrestrial connections so that the missing metadata can be accessed over the Internet, independently of the broadcast stream. The network can be used to access the Internet and make a connection with a service provider or a resolving authority or a broadcaster, using normal secure Internet mechanisms. There is a rich choice in standards that can be used for this. In cases where an Internet connection is not available over a network connection, the plain old telephone system (POTS) can be used, the Internet dialed up, metadata exchanged, and the line shut down. This really is a legacy method—the future is in "always on" connections via, for example, digital subscriber line (DSL) connections.

This kind of development is particularly suited as well to interactive TV programming, where many different delivery methods for both metadata and audio-visual data are being exploited, often using a combination of conventional digital delivery over air, by satellite, network streaming in real time, or downloading overnight. In these cases, the receiver must have the capability of storing the data and metadata so that everything can be brought together and synchronized when the program content needs it. As computer memory and storage get cheaper and computer processing power in home devices increases, the devices in a consumer's home now place no real limitation on content providers.

The most obvious and useful information to obtain over an Internet "metadata channel" is the electronic program guide or electronic content guide. EPGs or ECGs can be very simple, including just the program name and the time and channel information. But they can be made much more useful by carrying additional metadata. The guide can contain all kinds of information, such as the following:

- A short synopsis/summary
- A longer synopsis/summary
- Additional background information on a documentary or educational program
- Parental control content alert
- The intention of the program
- The format of the program
- Its genre (which is called content in the TV-Anytime specification)
- Origination information about the location where the program was produced
- The intended audience
- The atmosphere of a program
- The media type available
- Where to obtain the content

Alerts for programs not yet produced can be sent and used to record the program whenever it is transmitted in the future so that the consumer can add this program to his or her "like to see" list, and the box will automatically resolve the time, date, and channel information when it becomes available and start recording. This mechanism was intentionally developed by the TV-Anytime forum to create the possibility of alerting people to content that would interest them without giving away the transmission information, therefore making it impossible for competitors to schedule competing programs at the same time on other channels. This feature will be discussed later in this chapter.

A rich set of ECG metadata can highlight the differences between merely digitizing the traditional TV system and the digital TV service wanted and needed by the discerning consumer. With the overwhelming volume of content and TV channels already being delivered to the home, the consumer will likely need, and be willing to pay for, filters and facilities like those the ECGs can offer. If a broadcaster or service provider cannot or will not pass the information to the consumer, market forces dictate that the gap will be filled by more aggressive information companies with resultant mergers and takeovers of those companies who fall behind. Therefore it will be of increasing importance for content providers to feed the consumer with as much appropriate information as possible. If this is going to be done in a cost-efficient way, it is very important to collect the relevant metadata during the whole production chain, carrying this metadata through the workflow and on to the end consumer. Trying to find money for extra personnel to rekey metadata into the correct format for distribution to the consumer is probably a nonstarter! And if the original program creators do not supply the metadata, someone else will "produce it" by viewing the content and making a lot of guesses. The commercial implications and the resulting issues between program creators and listings companies or ECG suppliers are well out of the scope of this book.

The range of content available to consumers is becoming overwhelming, with content already coming over many delivery channels. Consumers need control over their TV watching time and therefore control over their recording device. A rich and accurate electronic content guide is a key component in meeting this need. This ECG should have a real-time "connection" with the transmitting broadcaster or service provider, at least for a period around the actual transmission time of the content, so that the actual start and stop information can come from the broadcast stream and be as up to date, and hence as accurate, as possible. Doing this will mean that programs that start early or late will be captured as a whole and not stop just before the vital climax of the program. Dealing with commercials within and around a program clearly has to be considered, and the TV-Anytime specifications leave a lot of room to do so imaginatively.

Metadata as the Connector between Broadcast Content and Internet Content

The availability of broadband Internet connections to the home using techniques such as ADSL, cable, and fiber to the home is now growing at an ever faster rate. Digital TV services will utilize these delivery channels to augment the even broader TV network connection and to provide the consumer with more channels. Many of these will be on-demand channels, and all will offer enhanced services that will provide additional facilities and content to broadcast programs. At its simplest, this can be straightforward textual or augmented audiovisual content, but it will also be possible to store temporarily hidden information on the consumer device in advance of the actual broadcast taking place. Downloaded metadata and live transmitted metadata can then be used to connect the two sources and enrich the program—for example with in-depth information, game attributes, enhanced functionality, or even higher definition pictures. This principle has been developed and demonstrated in a European project called Synchronised and Scalable Audio Video Content Across NeTworks, or SAVANT.

During the lifetime of the project, the SAVANT group demonstrated that these technologies permit a viewer to receive television programs both anytime (i.e., independently of the broadcaster's time schedule) and anywhere, on many different types of terminals and display devices. However, here again this will need the capture of appropriate metadata during the production process as well as a well-organized connection with the end consumer's device. The project has proved the whole chain and demonstrated interesting applications (see www.savant.tv). For the consumer, this type of digital television service blurs the boundaries between different types of media and delivery and starts to merge them.

Although these types of services are still in the early stages of development, it will not be long before they are sufficiently mature to be implemented in the consumer space. This will give anyone who owns content a new opportunity to exploit it, because if one's archive holds good quality metadata in its database, then old pro-

Figure 6.1.

grams can be given a new lease of life as they become available for exploitation using the new functionality that the technology enables. The logo of the SAVANT project clearly shows the aim and functionality achieved (Figure 6.1).

The SAVANT project has since been followed up by two other projects in the European Commission research program: the Generic Media Framework for Interactive Television (GMF4iTV), which aims to develop and demonstrate an end-to-end platform enabling interactive services on moving objects and TV programs according to MHP standard, and the porTiVity project, which aims to develop portable interactivity solutions.

Metadata and Consumer Needs

When selling content to consumers in the new era of digital content delivery, providers need to find ways to attract consumers to their content. To make advanced functionality readily accessible or even transparently available to the consumer, good quality and well-managed metadata will be essential. Currently, the group that is probably the most advanced in defining a suitably rich set of metadata along with the associated business models is the TV-Anytime (TVA) forum mentioned earlier. Much of the functionality developed by the TVA forum has already been adopted by others. Over time and as developments in technology mature, options that are currently only theoretically possible in consumer devices will be adopted and implemented.

At this stage it is probably useful to describe some basic and generic metadata elements and mechanisms specific to the TV-Anytime project:

Attractor. A metadata element that is accessible by the consumer in order to aid in the content selection process, thus attracting the consumer

Content reference identifier (CRID). An identifier for content that is independent of that content's location

Location resolution. The process of establishing the address (location and time) of a specific content instance from its CRID

Segment. A continuous portion of a piece of content—for example, a single topic in a news program

Segmentation. The process of creating segments from a piece of content

Stages of the Production and Transmission Process Chains to the Consumer

TV-Anytime Metadata Data Model

Content Creation

The content creation process box represents the production of a piece of content or a complete program (Figure 6.2). During the program creation, information about the program may (and should) also be captured. The metadata is likely to be in a form that fits the house workflow management system. This format, or scheme, must be as complete as possible and preferably in a form that can easily and automatically be translated or mapped into a usable publication form.

Content Publishing

Once content has been created, the content is then available for publication by a content publisher. This could be, for example, as part of a broadcast service or as a publication on the Internet. The content publishing process defines instantiations of programs—in other words, one output from the content publishing process is information about *where* the program can be found. In the broadcast case, this means a schedule for the services that are published.

Metadata Editing

The metadata editing process takes raw information from the content creation and publishing processes and edits this into a form that is suitable for representing the content to the end consumer. The output of this process is edited metadata for the programs or metadata describing the location of these programs.

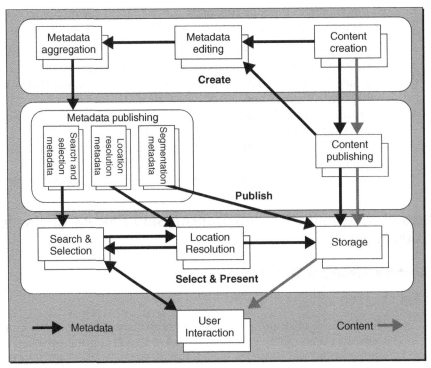

Figure 6.2. The flow of metadata and content through various stages of creation and up to the delivery to the end consumer. © ETSI 2004.[1]

Metadata Aggregation

To support a given TV-Anytime system, it is likely that metadata from a number of independent content creators and publishers will need to be aggregated. It is important to recognize that the process of metadata aggregation may result in the original metadata being changed.

Metadata Publishing

Regardless of whether a TV-Anytime system is completely open, so that a consumer has full choice in the range and combinations of networks, hardware and software platforms that can be used, or is restricted by the service provider to a limited range of options, an aggregated metadata set will need to be published to both the content selection and location resolution processes. The content selection process will be largely concerned with the metadata describing programs but may also involve use of the program location metadata. The location resolution service will simply require information about the location of programs.

---

[1] Further use, modification, or redistribution is strictly prohibited. ETSI standards are available from http://pda.etsi.org/pda and www.etsi.org/eds.

Content Selection

The content selection process may occur through the direct involvement of the consumer or may be performed on the consumer's behalf by a software agent. For a software agent to function correctly, metadata describing consumers and their preferences will need to be provided to the content selection process. This may be either inferred from the consumer's past history of content selection or by the explicit specification of preferences by the user (or a combination of the two). Note that the content selection process may be, in part, affected by knowledge of the program's location.

Location Resolution

The process of location resolution is simply one of discovering where (or when) a program can be found.

Metadata Elements

If content-providing organizations are going to take full advantage of available useful information to best make their content attractive to consumers, they will need to collect the metadata describing it and package it into a suitable schema. This schema could be one of the existing standard schemas or a subset created from one of those schemas. The best way of amassing the information is clearly to collect metadata as it first becomes available in the production workflow, and it seems logical, if a service based on the TV-Anytime specification is to be offered to consumers, to collect and use metadata elements based on that specification.

To give some idea of the richness of the dataset potentially achievable in such services, following is a list of just a few of the elements likely to be used. Further reading and deeper descriptions can be obtained from the specification (see www.tv-anytime.org) and the European Telecommunications Standards Institute (ETSI, www.etsi.org). At a minimum, content must be identified in some way, and the easiest and simplest identifier is the title. But a simple title will need to be supplemented in a way that will make the content attractive to the consumer and easy to purchase or to use.

The Content Reference ID (CRID)

All programs or groups of programs must have a meaningful title. Clearly, the title can be represented in different languages. However, the title is just about the minimum meaningful information about a program. To find information about programs and to localize the content, much more is needed, and the new features in consumer products provide some degree of intelligence to help the user to find content. The software in consumer products increasingly use "agents," which can make use of EPG structures to find programs, in much the same way that software "agents" currently crawl the Internet to elicit information. In the TV-Anytime specification, a much more sophisticated and user-centric method has been developed. Central to this process is the content reference identifier, the CRID. The CRID makes it possible to decouple *content* from both *channel* and *time*. In the resolving processes, it resolves channel and time to record the whereabouts and availability in time of a particular piece of content. The CRID will be key in the context of attracting people to any content that falls within the definitions of each consumer's own profile. Therefore, the metadata to create and operate the CRID is very important in terms of locating the content once a consumer has been attracted to it, and equally the metadata to create the attractors themselves is very important.

Attractors

The need to attract the audience is not new. Traditional broadcasting has long used presentation trailers, listings, magazines, and even advertising hoardings. But as the number of channels and choices available increases exponentially with the introduction of the new technologies, the potential number of consumers does not. The need to attract the audience to content using trailers, images, short descriptions of a program, or any other audience-pulling device becomes much more important. In the TV-Anytime concept, such devices are called "attractors."

Attractors are therefore devised in a way that will enable the linking of a consumer's interest and the recording mechanism so that the content of interest will be available at the moment the content consumer wants to watch it but with no effort on the part of the consumer. If they are to be really effective, attractors will not only have to include the "normal" information about the content as used for production, storage, or merchandising, but they will also need to include other or extra metadata elements to allow the attractor to demonstrate to consumers why this particular content is more desirable than any of the others available.

The following is a list of useful extra metadata elements extracted from the TV-Anytime specification—but note this is only an extract and is by no means exhaustive. The TV-Anytime specification contains detailed information of how these elements are expected to be used and implemented. In addition, it describes all the elements necessary for implementing a basic electronic program guide (EPG).

Suggested Elements to Create Attractors

Awards granted to a program. The title of the award, award organization, year of the award or nomination, detailed information about the particular award(s) or nomination(s), category of the award or nomination, nominee, recipient.

The role of a participant in a program. Actors, characters, key talent, key characters, writer, composer, conductor.

The location and time of a production. The country in which the program was placed, the depicted date of the production, the actual creation coordinates (i.e., location), the depicted coordinates (i.e., location), location and time information about the production's original release.

A synopsis of the production.

Any language-related information. For example the languages of the country of origin and of the content; the spoken language, languages of printed subtitles, options for closed captions and descriptive audio, sign language, whether these are windowed in the material, availability of language support from another source such as Internet downloads or special channels.

The relationship with other programs or program groups. This can clearly be a helpful feature for software agents in identifying other content in a relevant interest area of a consumer; it includes metadata such as related material, how related, any media locator information, and promotional text.

Parental guidance information. Will become more and more important and require elements describing the target (or intended) audience and any sex or violence involved.

Copyright information. Specified by copyright notice.

Group information. Whether a production is a series, serial, or episode. There is a subtle difference between a series and a serial: a series is an unordered collection of programs that can be shown in any sequence, whereas a serial is an ordered collection of program episodes that has to be shown in the correct sequence in order to make sense. This can be complicated by having self-contained serials for different seasons—in which case, there may be a series of serials (e.g., *Neighbours* 2001 season, episodes "1 to n" and *Neighbours* 2004 season, episodes "1 to n"). In everyday use, these terms tend to be used interchangeably, so that an ongoing drama may be colloquially referred to as a series when it is in reality a serial. Group information will also include elements such as program concept—the editorial concept for a program from which more specific program versions have been derived (e.g., the concept of *Blood Runner* as opposed to *Blood Runner—The Director's Cut*) and program compilation—a collection of programs that uses segments from multiple episodes of a serial or series combined into a single program.

Media review information. The media review information provides third-party reviews of audiovisual content, such as a critic's review of a movie. Independent program reviews can be presented to users to aid them in program selection.

The published duration. The duration of the program as advertised, which may therefore include other material such as trailers or program junctions. The *actual* duration will be provided by the location resolution mechanism.

Segmentation information. Some specific program types contain segments that have no relationship to one another, other than being in the same program. Good examples are current affairs programs, news programs, or magazine programs where the program is made up of a sequence of quite distinct, self-contained items or packages. In homes with advanced TV sets, it will be possible to discriminate between these program segments and watch them as separate little packages of content in their own right. To facilitate this practice, the program information must include extra elements, such as the following:

- *Segment list.* The list of the segments in the segment information table.
- *Segment information.* Text that contains information related to each segment.
- *Segment group information.* Text that contains information about a group of segments.

Program classification elements. This section defines types and genres of material, often using established industry shorthand and formulas. It is recommended that all programs and series contain a meaningful set of classification elements.

Genre classification can be a difficult subject, as it depends on culture, organization, and subjectivity. In the TV-Anytime forum, more than 100 companies from around the world agreed to a common set of dimensions for the classifications. It is a hierarchical system, where each broad term has subelements and even narrower terms. The system can be used in textual mode or in key coding:

- Encoding of an item using all information as presented in the TVA dictionary:
  3. Content,
    3.1 Nonfiction
        3.1.2 Philosophies of life
            3.1.2.1 Nonreligious philosophies
                3.1.2.2.2 Humanism
- Encoding of the same item using textual description: *Content, Nonfiction, Philosophies of life, Nonreligious philosophies, Humanism*
- Encoding of the same item using key encoding: *3.1.2.2.2*

The first example arguably uses an overkill of information, but it is a complete copy of the dictionary and structure for this specific element so that no information is lost or can be confused. The second example preserves the structure and "string" of information. The last example only gives the key, and the meaning of that key must be resolved from the complete dictionary (which therefore has to be loaded in the consumer's device). But note that this method is very efficient in terms of the data count, which has to be conveyed between content provider and consumer. It is therefore likely to operate quickly and will avoid slowing down other data that are crucial to the picture or sound in time-critical situations.

The TV-Anytime program classification is based on the following fields:

Intention. The content provider's apparent primary intention in publishing the program.

Format. Classifies programs according to their formal structure—in other words: how does the program look, regardless of the subject with which the program is dealing.

Content. Classifies programs according to their content or subject; often (and confusingly) wrongly called "genre."

Origination. How the program was originally originated—for example, from a concert hall or a studio.

Intended audience. Program intended for special audiences defined by age, cultural/ethnic background, profession, or other demographics.

Content alert. Warnings regarding the suitability of the content for different audiences.

Media type. The technical parameters of the source of the material making up the program.

Atmosphere. The terms used in the atmosphere dimension are intended to convey the key sense or feeling of the content.

The intention dimension, for example, contains terms such as "entertainment," "information," and "education" that describe the aim of the program at the conceptual phase. This can be useful for classifying early transmitted "attractors," which may be made available to consumers long before the program has been completed.

To help the consumer choose content, the program classification can be used in a multifield way, and each program can use one or more classification terms in each field. For example, all the fields can have classification terms assigned to a specific program and those terms can then appear in the consumer's selection window, the exception being content alert metadata, which inhibits the displaying of any information. Many more examples can be found in the TV-Anytime specification.

Metadata for Locating the "Stuff"

As noted earlier, in the new era of digital media the consumer is likely to be overwhelmed with content. Futuristic consumer products are already connected to different media transports such as cable, satellite, terrestrial, and broadband. Applications will of necessity only present content to the consumer in a user-friendly way—indeed, in the ideal case consumers will not need to know over which transport the content will arrive at their homes. To build this level of service, all of the metadata outlined earlier—plus probably more, yet unknown, metadata—will be needed in the near future. The important building blocks will be the ones that connect the consumer's choice with real broadcast or on-demand content.

To enable the connection between choice (which is really a choice of program concepts) and where the content is available, the TV-Anytime group developed the CRID mechanism outlined earlier. Usually, the CRID refers to a piece of content, though in some cases it may refer to one or more other CRIDs—for example, when content is available in more than one place, more than one channel, or at more

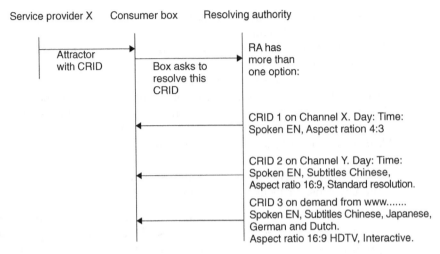

Figure 6.3.

than one time. It is logical, therefore, that the CRID can also act as the link that connects different content-related metadata descriptions.

Figure 6.3 demonstrates just one example of the many possibilities available when using the CRID and does not mean that delivery over the Internet has more options than sending over other channels. All kinds of combinations are possible.

A fundamental key feature of a CRID is that it makes it possible to find content that will be available in the future as well as content on a given channel at a specific time. It essentially points to an authority that resolves the information and sends appropriate information, current at that moment, back to the consumer device. Such information might, for example, be a message: "Come back in four months time and I can tell you more." The consumer application can take care of the process from then on so that the consumer who had clicked on a trailer or attractor will know that the specific content will be recorded on the system when it becomes available. Using the metadata mentioned already in combination with the mechanism of the TV-Anytime CRID, sophisticated applications can be built, forming the basis for a strong relationship between content providers and consumers and thus building a resilient business model.

Metadata in Marketing

If producers were to create program material just for their own fun or satisfaction and then keep it secret from the rest of the world, they could manage with very simple and limited metadata—just the information needed to find the material on their own private shelf.

However, keeping program material secret and to themselves is something professional producers and program makers very seldom do! They want (and need) to sell their programs to publishers, packaging companies, or direct to consumers. The program therefore needs to be advertised, and the information about the program has to be made available to the widest possible number of potential purchasers. The TV-Anytime CRID is heavily based on the availability of information about content and about all the different versions of that content.

Global database structures where content creators and version creators can make available information about content and all its versions do not really exist at the moment. But using the CRID does not mean that all content from all over the world has to be submitted to one enormous database. Various standardization groups have already developed the methodologies and building blocks to create structures where databases can "talk" to each other and expose the version or original content that will be available from a given owner, creator, publisher, or distributor. The International Standard Audio-visual Number (ISAN) specification (www.isan.org) already offers tools to enable this methodology, and the ISAN organization not only has its own space on the World Wide Web but also has a registered uniform resource locator (isan://). Similarly, TV-Anytime has registered "crid://" as a uniform resource locator which

> has been devised to allow references to current or future scheduled publications of broadcast media content over television distribution platforms and the Internet.
>
> The initial intended application is as an embedded link within scheduled programme description metadata that can be used by the home user or agent to associate a programme selection with the corresponding programme location information for subsequent automatic acquisition.
>
> The "CRID:" Uniform Resource Locator is designed to be the bridge between programme-related descriptive metadata and corresponding programme location data that may be published over a different distribution network or at a different time.

Added Value for the Viewer

The added value for the viewer is simple—people can find content in the version they want, when they want it.

Added Information for Marketers

Added value for marketers is also simple—they know where potential consumers will look for content and then guide consumers to version they are looking for.

The marketing mechanism can do the work here and sift out unreliable or misleading suppliers of information. Consumers will, in the end, always find the way to those parties they trust.

Other Useful Metadata

In addition to metadata for attracting consumers to content and marketing metadata, there are other valuable elements of metadata. Some are useful for searching, and some are useful for playing the content once it has been located.

Modification Date

The modification date describes when the audiovisual work was last modified. This is beneficial in tracking back through alternative versions when trying to understand in what order they were created, and it is also useful if the original creation date is available. This is especially relevant if a work has been updated or reversioned because some new evidence or documentation has come to light or because a character or story has developed.

However, it may be the case that certain versions had almost identical creation dates, especially if they were being versioned as part of a co-production deal and thus made within days or even hours of each other. Then the order in which this work is completed happens for economic, not content, reasons.

Audio and Video Information

This section specifies the type and arrangement of the video and audio elements as well as any processing carried out on them, along with the industry standards used for the processing, and patented techniques.

File Information

File information includes several key elements:

FileFormat. Specifies the file type of the different formats available from different sources (for example, AC3, DTS, MP3, MPEG-1, MPEG-2 Layer III, MPEG-2 AAC, MPEG-4 part 10). This will affect parameters such as high or low definition, movement rendering, whether suitable for viewing on a large screen or on a small mobile screen, and so on.

File size. Specifies the overall length of the file as data, in bytes.

VisualCoding. Defines the aspect ratios of shooting and presentation, and the basic image characteristics, pixel height and width, and whether the image is color or black and white, and so on.

AudioCoding.

And so on . . .

Clearly, these are only examples of metadata that might typically by used in a future consumer application, and the above list is by no means complete or exhaustive. In practice, the metadata used will depend on the business model used in deriving and offering a product or service—and this book cannot detail all of the possible business models. The TV-Anytime specification (especially its first chapter) has typical possible business models worked out and can provide further reading.

TV-Anytime–compliant devices are variously referred to as the personal video recorder (PVR) or the digital video recorder (DVR). These PVR/DVR devices are highly attractive to consumers in their own right as straightforward recorders, but they become much more desirable when used in conjunction with a service built on the use of descriptive metadata. Helping consumers to satisfy their viewing needs effortlessly while at the same time providing an accurate and well-managed service will be an attraction in itself. But there always is a drawback in good things. As Johan Cruiyf, a Dutch soccer player, said, "Every advantage has got its own disadvantage." The disadvantage with these kinds of consumer devices is that individuals are able to hop through a program and ruin the director's carefully crafted work. And this functionality can also be used to skip commercials—hardly likely to be popular with advertisers! Every consumer will want to have such a facility, but, rightly or wrongly, it is unlikely to be popular in the broadcast/service provider world. In fact, it is entirely possible that metadata will also be used to inhibit such a facility, although in practice skipping commercials has always happened—commercial breaks provide viewers with an opportunity to get something from the kitchen or make a quick phone call, for example. The TV-Anytime specification provides for many variations on the themes of hopping through a program and skipping commercials, supported by all manner of metadata.

Recent studies by the major USA networks have also shown that people using a PVR/DVR watch more TV per day and watch more commercials than people without such a device—while skipping through the commercials they sometimes jump back to watch a particular commercial if it falls within their interest window or if it is just plain humorous and appeals to them. This may well turn out to be reason enough for some vendors to start Commercial On Demand services!

In summary, the continuing evolution of the convergence between traditional broadcast and the Internet as means of delivering programs will lead eventually from multinetwork broadcasting solutions to multiservice Internet-Protocol solutions using rich metadata as the key enabler.

7 Metadata in Public Collections

Most of this book up to now has concentrated on metadata created by the makers or owners of the work. When television programs or newsfilm are donated to public collections, metadata creation then becomes the responsibility of the caretaking organization. The organization will need to save relevant legacy metadata that perhaps was received with the physical tapes or films, but it must also add content, preservation, and provenance data, following standardized cataloging rules.

University and national libraries and archives can sometimes hold individual programs, series, or, in the case of some local television stations in the United States, entire broadcasting collections. This chapter is not concerned with individual programs and series commercially distributed by broadcasters; their provenance is clear. Instead, we will focus on programs donated to public archives or libraries by either the stations themselves or by individuals or production companies.

The importance of preserving television and broadcasting history as a public imperative was first recognized by public archives, not by the broadcasters. Networks might save their early raw news footage because of its reuse (and resale) value, but their footage libraries are for their own use—not for public research. Public archives consider the programs to be important cultural documentation that should be available to all and, in the case of local newsfilm, historical documentation of a region's events that would not necessarily be disseminated on the national network news. Early entertainment programs were ephemeral transmissions, sometimes captured as kinescopes (film recordings) in the pre-videotape era. In the United States, television programs from the 1950s are often not found at the corporate station archives but at places like the Library of Congress, the University of California Los Angeles (UCLA) Film and Television Archive, and the University of Georgia Peabody Awards Archive. Complete programs can be found at these archives as the result of copyright deposits (in the case of the Library of Congress), or deposits from the stations or donations from people involved in the production. In the Netherlands, the national archive Beeld and Geluid holds material given to them by the public broadcasting organizations. However, there is usually no mandatory requirement for broadcasters to give material to the national archive and many have their own archive, which includes material that they do not want to make public.

The public archives preserve, catalog, and provide access to the programs they acquire. Metadata (cataloging records) should retain legacy data provided by the broadcaster, but the cataloger will also add data such as names and subject headings as well as rights, technical, and preservation information. The resulting record can be an interesting hybrid of data created by the broadcaster (usually not following standards) morphed into a clean, standardized catalog record. The metadata has evolved into something useful to the archive but far from its origins.

Donations by Broadcasters

Newsfilm

The most common type of programming donated or deposited to public collections directly by broadcasters is 16mm newsfilm shot between the 1950s to early 1970s (entertainment and educational or documentary programs tend to be donated by individuals who were involved in the production). Before $^3/_4$″ U-matic portable videocassettes were manufactured beginning in 1971, all newsfilm shot on location in the United States was captured on 16mm reversal film. In Europe, 35mm film was sometimes used for black and white footage, while color footage was usually shot in 16mm. Reversal stock allowed for fast processing and editing in time for the evening news broadcast. There was no need to wait for a negative to be processed and a positive print struck; when processed, the reversal film came out positive. This meant that the newsfilm was unique. The physical film that was shot in the field is what was used in the edited program—no other copies existed.

Film could be shot silent as B-roll or filmed using an Auricon camera which captured an optical soundtrack on the reversal film. In the late 1960s and early 1970s, magnetic stripes were added to the reversal stock so that sound was captured on the magnetic stripe rather than the optical track. Many European broadcasters used $^1/_4$″ tape locked to the film camera and then transferred the audio to 16mm magnetic track.

After cutting out the brief segments for use in the news program, the small 400-foot film rolls were spliced with other rolls to form 1600-foot reels. As with motion picture newsreels of the 1920s through 1940s, the only cataloging done was to create index cards or files describing the reel. The cards noted particularly good segments and listed the date, location, event, and people included in the reel.

By the time U-matic videocassettes arrived in the early 1970s, active television stations found themselves with warehouses filled with thousands of 16 mm cans and boxes and $\frac{1}{4}$" tapes. Room had to be made for the videocassettes, so many local broadcasters threw the films away. A report on the state of American television preservation conducted in 1997 by the Library of Congress estimates that only 15 percent of newsfilm shot by local stations survives today[1]—and most of that footage exists because the film was donated to universities.

Sometimes the local stations signed over their rights to the footage to the university, which allowed the university to charge license fees for sales of clips. The earned income from sales can help fund preservation efforts. But in order to sell the footage, there must be shot-list metadata so clips can be searched and retrieved. If the newsfilm was not acquired with a database, then the public institution must either transcribe the index cards into a database, or create the data from scratch—a far more time-consuming enterprise.

Because of its uniqueness and the deterioration tendencies of film and early U-matic cassettes, broadcast material such as newsfilm will require extensive information beyond describing the expected content. Information describing the physical nature of the item should be included, as this can give hints to future preservation problems. For example, 16 mm newsfilm with a magnetic sound stripe will be prone to vinegar syndrome at a faster rate than its silent or optical track comrades, due to the iron in the magnetic stripe attracting moisture and thus accelerating acetate deterioration in the film. It will be important to note that the film has a magnetic stripe in the cataloging record, so the archivists can monitor the film and perhaps put it in colder storage than other reels to slow down the deterioration process.

Current Affairs Programs and Documentaries

Current affairs and other time-sensitive programs are frequently not saved in broadcasters' archives. These programs on topics relevant to the day's news are often transmitted live, with perhaps a tape or kinescope recording for short-term archiving. Broadcasters might not find value in storing the programs when the "current affairs" have long passed their currency, and the recordings can eventually find themselves donated to a public archive. Just as 25-year-old local news-

---

[1] *Television and Video Preservation 1997: A Study of the Current State of American Television and Video Preservation: Report of the Librarian of Congress.* Washington, DC: Library of Congress, 1997. Vol. 1: Report.

film can have value to students, scholars, and educators researching an area's history, so can these current affairs programs shed light on topics that were important at a particular moment in time. The public archives will add metadata on the subjects discussed, people interviewed, and airdate. The tapes or kinescopes will often be unique copies, so preservation information will be added as well.

Donations by Individuals and Production Companies

Individuals and production companies associated with programs tend to donate their personal copies of entertainment programs with which they were involved. Donations can include single programs or series. Usually there are no legacy data other than what is written on the tape container or film can. While the individual donated the physical copy, the intellectual property rights still remain with the copyright holder: the network, station, or production company.

If no data are donated along with the physical programs, the cataloger must create the data from scratch. The cataloger will usually conduct research about the program or series in reference books and add any information to the record that can be gleaned from viewing the program (cast and technical credits, subject content, etc.).

Programs Recorded Off-Air

Some national archives in Europe and university archives in the United States record programs off-air for permanent or limited archiving. Recorded programs are usually news broadcasts, although some organizations record a station's 24-hour transmission. For instance, the British Film Institute records programs off-air, the national archive in the Netherlands records the daily transmission of the three public networks from the transmission feeds (note that they record the public networks only, not the private commercial ones), and there are similar arrangements in France and other countries. In the United States, off-air recording by nonprofit educational organizations for educational use is allowed.

Of course, recordings captured from feeds do not come with any metadata, so the public archive must create it. The catalog record usually contains minimal information, often just a title field with the station, program title, and airdate such as "CBS Evening News. 2005-07-27," with another field giving the tape location on the shelf.

Metadata Added by the Public Archive

Adapting Legacy Metadata

The most common type of production donated to public archives is local television newsfilm, which is also the most likely to have some form of legacy data since it was in the broadcaster's best interests to immediately find its own footage for the nightly news. Index cards or databases in now-extinct applications can contain shotlist records describing specific clips on the reels. At a minimum, the information should include the date, location, and a brief description of the shot. Cataloging records for raw newsfilm have a different data structure than those for complete broadcast programs. They tend to be brief, with keywords for the content the primary focus. "Keywords" are names, topical words or phrases, and geographic locations—all taken from a controlled vocabulary.

If a database exists, it was created by the forward-thinking station staff who transcribed data from cards so the station could quickly search for needed "historical" footage. Databases have the greater likelihood to contain names and topical content terms (events, subjects, etc.). However, the database will often live in an early application that has not been manufactured for 20 years, so before anything can be done with it, the data must be coaxed out and passed through data conversion scripts until it achieves a usable form. Fields or parsed data are then mapped to the archive's database structure for enhancement by cataloging staff.

Shotlist cataloging utilizing keywords does not lend itself to elegant Machine-Readable Cataloging (MARC) records. Archives and libraries with these materials tend to create one creation-level record for the library online catalog that describes the newsfilm in general and lets users know where they can go to find more information. The keyworded shot records would be stored in a separate, standalone database (often in an off-the-shelf product like Filemaker Pro or Microsoft Access). At the request of the user, staff might search the standalone shotlist database for desired footage, print the results, and retrieve the tapes or DVDs with the desired clips. Few public archives have digitized their newsfilm collections and made them available on the Internet, which would allow users to search for and retrieve footage on their own.

Tracking History and Provenance

Ideally, the public organization will try to include the history of the creation of the footage or program, and how it acquired the program, in the cataloging record. This should be done even if acquisition or provenance fields are suppressed from public access. Staff in 5, 20, 50 and more years will need to know how the particular programs came under the safekeeping of the public archive, outside the walls of the broadcasting company.

Preservation Metadata

If the public archive preserves the program or footage, those actions should be noted in the cataloging record. For films tested with acid detection strips, the date of the test and results should be noted in the individual records. Problems with the physical medium—film deterioration, color fading, video dropouts, and so forth—should be included in the record, as well as the date of last inspection. Any transfers or reformatting should be described, including the date of transfer, who did it, and to what format the work was transferred. The unique identifier for the reformatted copy made from the original should be specified so that the provenance of the copy is clear.

Intellectual Property

Acquisition information (how the public archive came to acquire the programs) is different from intellectual property information, which identifies the known copyright holders of the works. Here is where the archive could note that rights were transferred from the broadcaster to the archive or that the broadcaster, production company, or other entity holds the rights. Sometimes links to the rights-holder's permission web pages can be included in the public cataloging record, taking the interested user directly to a place where footage can be licensed.

Including rights information in the metadata record can be tricky. If the cataloger is not absolutely certain about who owns the rights to the program, it is best to not include that information at all or to present the information as simply quoting what is on the tape or film itself so it is "historical" research information. If the provided rights ownership information is wrong but asserted as being accurate, the public archive could find itself in legal trouble. Of course, it is up to the user to keep up to date on changing copyright laws in the country of origin and in the country of use.

Getting Metadata out to the Public

Public archives that hold broadcasting programs are frequently part of universities, which already have established online catalogs. The cataloging records follow standard cataloging rules such as AACR2 and AMIM2 (discussed in Chapter 3) and use national name authorities (the Library of Congress Name Authority File [LCNAF]). These online catalogs can be publicly accessible on the Internet, or at the very least the records are available to other academic institutions. While the items themselves usually cannot leave the archive premises, the cataloging records can provide useful information describing the program and its history—information of value to researchers and broadcasters alike. An example of a public archive record that follows library standards can be found in Appendix 1. The UCLA Film and Television Archive is the archive for the Hallmark Hall of Fame series of made-for-television movies and specials. The sample record for the program *The Price* is offered in both MARC format and in the general display that users would find on the university's campus (Figure 7.1).

Figure 7.1. George C. Scott and Colleen Dewhurst in the Hallmark Hall of Fame presentation of Arthur Miller's *The Price.* Originally broadcast on February 3, 1971.

When large collections are donated to an archive and no staff members are available to individually catalog every item, the archive can opt instead to create a "finding aid." The finding aid describes the history of the collection, how it was acquired, and "box level" basic descriptions of items contained in specific boxes (e.g., "6:00 News broadcasts, 1999-01-01 to 1999-02-01"). Finding aids follow a definite structure proscribed by the archival profession. They are often encoded in Encoded Archival Description (EAD) and placed on the library's or archive's website.

Appendix 1 Sample Metadata Records

This appendix presents examples of PBCore implementation at two public television stations in the United States; one example of cataloging raw news footage; and MARC and public displays of a record for an entertainment program held by a public archive. All records date from September 2005. Websites where other sample records can be found are listed at the end of the appendix.

PBCore

Kentucky Educational Television

Kentucky Educational Television (KET) and Wisconsin Public Television provided sample PBCore records (Figure A1.1). KET supplied two screen shots from its File-makerPro database for a record of an edited, broadcast program. The first screen shot shows a display with all the metadata fields in the KET database. Several fields, or "buckets" of data, are described as being automatically ingested into the system.

The second screen shot shows the data entry screen for the cataloger (Figure A1.2). The cataloger enters content information about the specific clip or program into the record, which is consolidated into the full record.

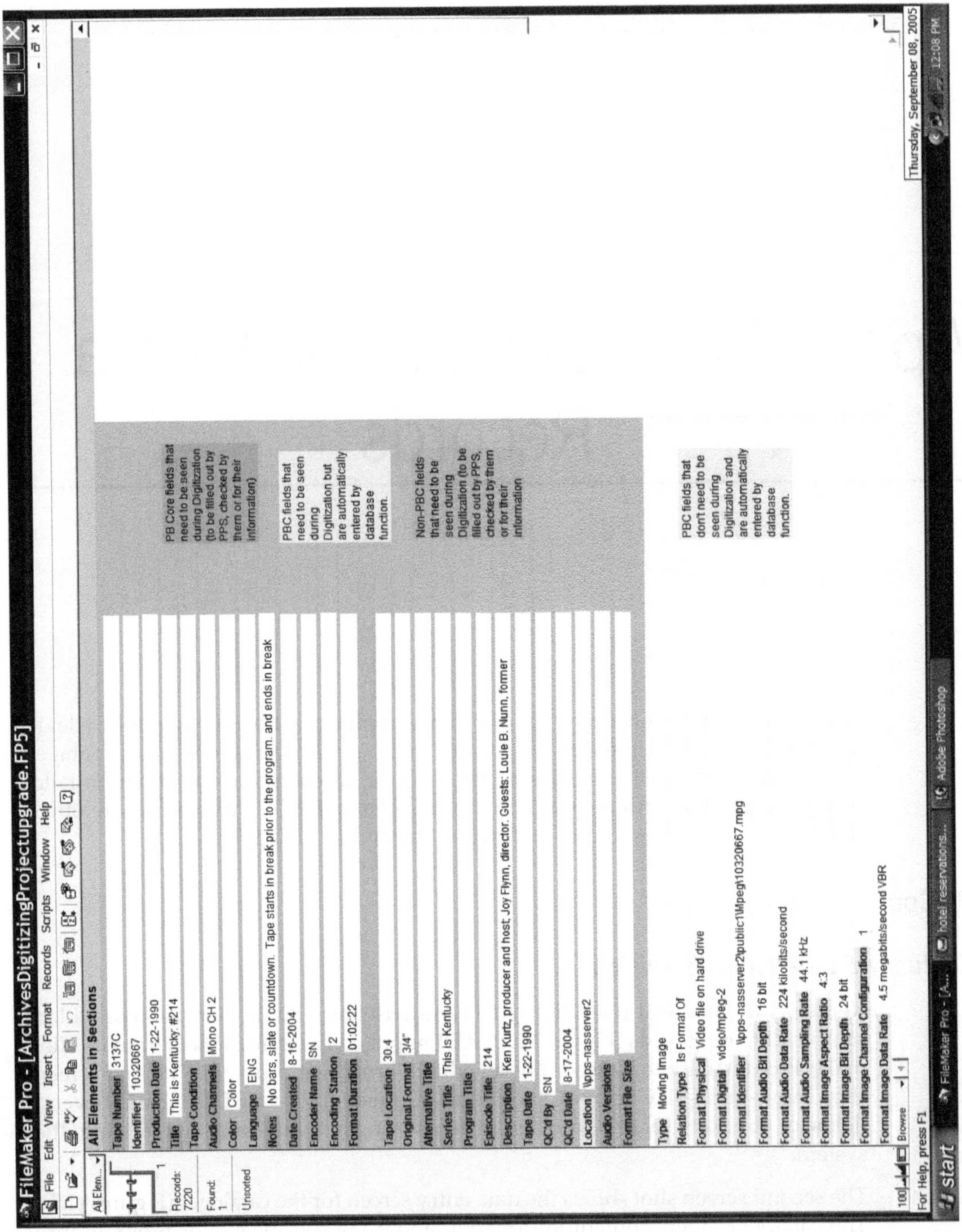

FileMaker Pro - [ArchivesDigitizingProjectupgrade.FP5]

File Edit View Insert Format Records Scripts Window Help

All Elements in Sections

Records: 7220

Found: 1

Unsorted

Tape Number 3137C

Identifier 10320667

Production Date 1-22-1990

Title This is Kentucky #214

Tape Condition

Audio Channels Mono CH 2

Color Color

Language ENG

Notes No bars, slate or countdown. Tape starts in break prior to the program. and ends in break

Date Created 8-16-2004

Encoder Name SN

Encoding Station 2

Format Duration 01:02:22

Tape Location 30.4

Original Format 3/4"

Alternative Title

Series Title This is Kentucky

Program Title

Episode Title 214

Description Ken Kurtz, producer and host. Joy Flynn, director. Guests: Louie B. Nunn, former

Tape Date 1-22-1990

QC'd By SN

QC'd Date 8-17-2004

Location Npps-nasserver2

Audio Versions

Format File Size

Type Moving Image

Relation Type Is Format Of

Format Physical Video file on hard drive

Format Digital video/mpeg-2

Format Identifier \\pps-nasserver2\public1\Mpeg\10320667.mpg

Format Audio Bit Depth 16 bit

Format Audio Data Rate 224 kilobits/second

Format Audio Sampling Rate 44.1 kHz

Format Image Aspect Ratio 4:3

Format Image Bit Depth 24 bit

Format Image Channel Configuration 1

Format Image Data Rate 4.5 megabits/second VBR

PB Core fields that need to be seen during Digitization (to be filled out by PPS, checked by them or for their information)

PBC fields that need to be seen during Digitization but are automatically entered by database function.

Non-PBC fields that need to be seen during Digitization (to be filled out by PPS, checked by them or for their information

PBC fields that don't need to be seen during Digitization and are automatically entered by database function.

Thursday, September 08, 2005   12:08 PM

Start   FileMaker Pro - [A...   hotel reservations...   Adobe Photoshop

Figure A1.1.

114

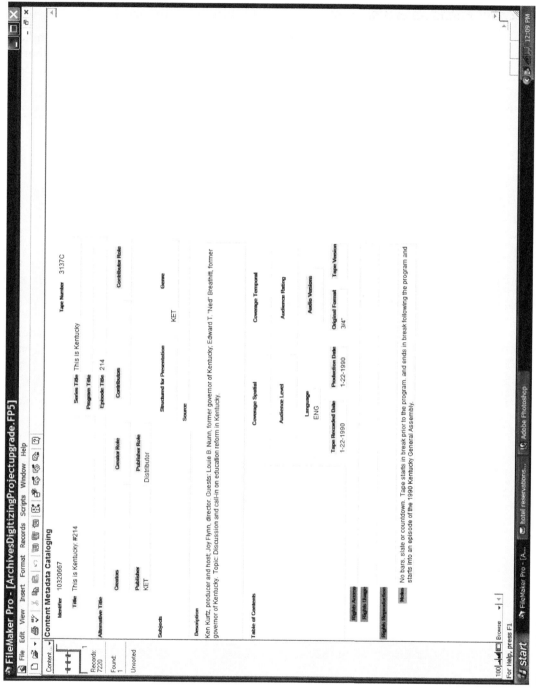

Figure A1.2.

Wisconsin Public Television

Wisconsin Public Television (WPTV) offers the following listing as an example of a record for a complete edited program. Note that the record states the authority for the subject headings used (the International Press Telecommunications Council [IPTC]).

Tape Number:	NPA IWB
Title:	In Wisconsin 332P
Title Type:	Series/Program
Program or Series Title:	In Wisconsin
Creator:	Bissen, Kathy//Executive Producer
	Sloan-Miller, Christine//Producer
Contributor:	Loew, Patty//Host
	Freyberg, Frederica//Producer
	Hackett, Art//Producer
	Gorman, Laurie//Producer
Date Created:	2005-05-12
Broadcast Date:	2005-05-12
Publisher:	Board of Regents UW//Copyright holder
	Education Communications Board//Copyright holder
	Wisconsin Public Television//Presenter
Subject:	children
	pediatrics
	organ donation
	arts, culture, and entertainment
	labor
	electricity production and distribution
	politics
	poetry
	death and dying
Subject Authority Used:	International Press Telecommunications Council

Description: Arrowhead Powerline (8:04)

The Arrowhead Weston power line connects electrical substations in Duluth, Minnesota and Wausau, Wisconsin. It's intended to improve electric reliability by providing a second path for power from the west. The line has been the subject of protests since it was proposed six years ago. While 12 miles of the line have already been built in Minnesota, the Douglas County Board is trying to block the line by forbidding use of county owned forest land. The line's owner, American Transmission Co., says the line will go in with or without county approval. Mark Williamson, Vice President American Transmission Co.; Mark Liebaert, Douglas Co. Supervisor; Doug Finn, Douglas Co. Board Chair; Woody Budnick, Douglas Co. Supervisor; Carl Sjodin

Producer: Art Hackett

Videographer: Bruce Johnson

Audio Recordist: Steve Aronson, Brad Wray

Editor: Wendy Woodard

Label Quilt (7:04)

Milwaukee artist Terese Agnew has devoted her latest work, Portrait of a Textile Worker, to make visible one worker among millions who make the things we as American consumers wear and use everyday. The quilt is based on a photo of a textile worker in Bangladesh by Charles Kernaghan and made entirely of garment labels contributed from people around the globe. Agnew's piece speaks to the human cost behind the designer labels.

Producer: Laurie Gorman

Dasha Kelly (7:03)

Dasha Kelly of Milwaukee suffered the worst tragedy a parent can experience . . . the loss of a child. Baby Chase was born with a rare and serious heart defect and lost his fight for life four months later. What makes the situation even more heartbreaking, is that baby Chase passed away while waiting for a heart transplant—an operation that may have saved his life.

Frederica Freyberg reports that Dasha Kelly dealt, in part, with the tragic loss of her son by working with Children's Hospital of Wisconsin to establish a memorial fund in his name, "Chase's Gift." The money raised will be used to help raise awareness of the dire need for pediatric organ donation. Doctors say that right now in Wisconsin five children are waiting for a donor heart and many others are awaiting other types of organ donations. Dr. Andrew Pelech, Cardiologist Children's Hospital of Wisconsin; Dr. Stuart Berger, Medical Director Children's Hospital of Wisconsin

Producer: Fredica Freyberg

Videographer: Butch Soetenga, Bruce Johnson

Editor: Mike Eicher

Postcard: waterfall in Governor Dodge State Park

Description Type:	Abstract
Format:	BetaSP
Format Aspect Ratio:	4:3
Format Generations:	Moving Image/Air Copy
Tape Location:	Media Library
Duration:	00:27:46
Format Colors:	Color
Genre:	Newsmagazine
Shoot Location/s:	Milwaukee, Wisconsin; Duluth, Minnesota; Rhinelander, Wisconsin; Marathon County, Solon Springs, Wisconsin
Date/Time Period:	November 2000, April 2002, April 2005, May 2005
Audience Level:	Other
Language:	eng (English)
Format Standard:	NTSC video
Date Of Record Release:	2005-05-16 11:50:30 (W3C-DTF)
Date Record Checked:	2005-05-16 (W3C-DTF)
Format Media Type:	Moving Image
Alternative Modes:	CC1 in English
Annotation:	Grantor: Alliant Energy
Identifier Source:	Wisconsin Public Television
Date of Record Creation:	2005-05-16 11:50:05 (W3C-DTF)
Date Last Modified:	2005-08-22 11:27:37 (W3C-DTF)

Raw News Footage Cataloging: CNN

This record is an example of raw news footage cataloging from the CNN Library in Atlanta. It is presented in two views: the view as users see it in CNN's digital library system and a version showing the data in field list format with descriptors.

The first view is a screen shot as the record appears to users (Figure A1.3). Under the Collection and Asset ID fields are three icons that users can click to access digital files. The first icon accesses the keyframe file, the second retrieves a low-resolution digital file, and the third retrieves a high-resolution digital video file.

The second view of the record shows the same data in a field list format. Added to this record are keywords supplied by catalogers from CNN's internal controlled vocabulary list of descriptors.

Date: 11/10/1989
Slug: TROOPS WALL
Country: EAST GERMANY
State:
City: EAST BERLIN
Type: RAW

Rec #	Date	Slug	Dateline	Type	Reporter	Length	Source	Tape #	Record ID#
1 □	11/10/1989	TROOP S WALL	EAST GERMANY; EAST BERLIN;	RAW		00:06:06:15	CNN	B2226#015	2001010093317

Collection : Atlanta **Asset ID :** 90137249

Video Config:	**Audio Config:**	**Tape Format:** BETA	**Offsite Box#:**

Abstract: East German troops watch as crowd celebrates end of Berlin Wall.

Description: 00:50:30:10 pan soldiers to WS large crowd :37/ pan military truck, soldiers :13/ pan troops facing people on wall to crowd & guards below :35/ WS crowd chanting :18/ pan to Brandenburg Gate then people below :11/ troops standing in line :10/ WS crowd chant at soldiers :26/ CU people climb wall towards camera on top of wall :21/ pan to WS Brandenburg Gate :09/ WS troops face wall, help people climb :32/ pan line of soldiers :12/ men chisel crack in wall -- hear sound of chiseling:26/ CU man chisels wall and looks through crack :18/ VS cameraman in crowd shooting video :26/ CU military gun turret light goes on then pan to guards :41/ WS Brandenburg Gate & troops :32 (6:06) /

Figure A1.3.

Length: 00:06:06:15
Source: CNN
Tape #: B2226#015
Record ID#: 90137249
Collection: ATLANTA
Tape Format: BETA

Abstract: East German troops watch as crowd celebrates end of Berlin Wall.

Description:

pan soldiers to WS large crowd :37/ pan military truck, soldiers :13/ pan troops facing people on wall to crowd & guards below :35/ WS crowd chanting :18/ pan to Brandenburg Gate, then people below :11/ troops standing in line :10/ WS crowd chants at soldiers :26/ CU people climb wall towards camera on top of wall :21/ pan to WS Brandenburg Gate :09/ WS troops face wall, help people climb :32/ pan line of soldiers :12/ men chisel crack in wall—hear sound of chiseling :26/ CU man chisels wall and looks through crack :18/ VS cameraman in crowd shooting video :26/ CU military gun turret light goes on then pan to guards :41/ WS Brandenburg Gate & troops :32

EAST BERLIN; EAST GERMANY; BERLIN WALL; BRANDENBURG GATE; REUNIFI-CATION; COLD WAR; POLITICAL REFORM; WEST BERLIN; WEST GERMANY; SOLDIERS [EAST GERMANY]; DEMOLITION; CROWDS; CHANTING; CHISELS; CLIMBING; CRACKS; CELEBRATIONS; CAMERA CREWS

CNN Library Metadata Dictionary (Field List)

The sample record on the fall of the Berlin Wall does not show all metadata fields available to catalogers. The CNN Library has kindly supplied its entire metadata dictionary, or field list, representing all possible fields that can contain data:

Slug:

Collection:

Asset ID:

Date:

Source:

Type:

Length:

Division:

Broad Category:

Country:

State:

City:

County:

Other Geo:

Reporter:

Abstract:

Misc Notes:

ImageSource Licensable:

Restriction:

Market Embargo:

Archive Comp #:

Cassette #:

Tape Format:

Tape Start:

Type Category:

Video Config:

Audio Config:

Music Ind:

Music Code:

Video Tape Status:

Video Tape State:

Offsite Box #:

Transfer Instructions:

Drop Frame:

Ingest Duration:

Ingest Source:

DTF Group:

Feed Point:

Feed Start:

Feed End:

Receiver:

Technical Quality:

Cut From:

Anchor/Host:

Editor:

Producer:

Photographer:

Audio Tech:

Aired On CNN:

Aired On HDLN:

Aired On CNNI:

Fonts:

Package Script:

Show Script:

Speech:

Closed Caption:

OCR:

Creation Date:

Created By:

Ingested By:

Ingested On:

Logged By:

Logged On:

Indexed By:

Indexed On:

Updated By:

Updated On:

Legacy ID:

Entertainment Program in MARC

The University of California Los Angeles (UCLA) Film and Television Archive catalogs its collections in MARC format as described in Chapters 3 and 7. Their record for the Hallmark Hall of Fame program *The Price* is offered here in both MARC and a general display for comparisons. The 700 MARC fields are names associated with the program, with the data values taken from the Library of Congress Name Authority File (LCNAF).

The Price: MARC Record

000 03007cgm a2200529 a 450
001 46411
005 20050919133743.0
008 t19711970xxu090 mleng d
033 01 |a 197102031930
035 __ |9 04-AAE-6536
040 __ |a CLU |c CLU
130 0_ |a Hallmark hall of fame (Television program). |p Price.
245 00 |a Hallmark hall of fame. |p Arthur Miller's The price / |c a Talent
Associates, Norton Simon, Inc. production in association with the National

Broadcasting Company ; produced with the NBC-TV Network ; Hallmark Cards ; producer, David Susskind ; director, Fielder Cook.

260 __ |a United States : |b NBC, |c [1971-02-03], c1970.

500 __ |a Play; anthology.

500 __ |a "Adapted by Arthur Miller from his own play"–Television drama series programming, 1959–1975 / Larry James Gianakos.

511 1_ |a Starred George C. Scott as Victor Franz; co-starred Barry Sullivan as Walter Franz; David Burns as Gregory Solomon and Colleen Dewhurst as Esther Franz.

508 __ |a Associate producer, Alan Shayne. Art director, John Clements. Costumes, Ann Roth; assistant to the director, Enid Roth. Lighting director, Jim Boyers; unit manager, Albert Tolley. Floor manager, John Linton; production assistant, Mary Dalison. Production secretary, Pamela Susskind. Music composed by Arthur Rubinstein; music produced by Score Productions Inc. Recorded at Intertel Colour Television Ltd. Studios, England.

500 __ |a Originally broadcast Wednesday evening, February 3, 1971, 7:30 to 9:00 p.m., according to Television drama series programming, 1959–1975 / Larry James Gianakos.

500 __ |a Original format: videotape.

505 8_ |a Commercials: Hallmark Valentine's Day cards—Hallmark Valentine's Day cards—Hallmark party accessories—Hallmark writing instruments—Hallmark writing papers—Hallmark Cards—Hallmark Cards.

500 __ |a Copyright notice on film: c1970 Talent Associates-Norton Simon, Inc.

655 _7 |a Plays. |2 mim

655 _7 |a Anthologies. |2 mim

700 1_ |a Miller, Arthur, |d 1915- |t Price.

700 1_ |a Susskind, David, |d 1920- |e production

700 1_ |a Cook, Fielder, |d 1923- |e direction

700 1_ |a Shayne, Alan. |e production

700 1_ |a Clements, John. |e production design

700 1_ |a Roth, Ann. |e production design

700 1_ |a Rubinstein, Artur, |d 1887- |e music

700 1_ |a Scott, George C., |d 1927- |e cast

700 1_ |a Sullivan, Barry, |d 1912- |e cast

700 1_ |a Burns, David, |d 1902–1971. |e cast

700 1_ |a Dewhurst, Colleen. |e cast

710 2_ |a Talent Associates.

710 2_ |a Norton Simon Inc.

710 2_ |a National Broadcasting Company, inc.

710 2_ |a NBC Television Network.

710 2_ |a Hallmark Cards, Inc.

730 02 |a Commercials. Hallmark.

246 3_ |a Price.

246 3_ |**a** Arthur Miller's the price.
901 __ |**a** HHF |**b** Hallmark Collection
901 __ |**a** TV |**b** Television Collection
910 __ |**a** Cataloged April 22, 1988, jm; rev. April 13, 2001, my; rev. September 19, 2005, my.
935 __ |**a** FA0008385

The Price: **General Public Display**

Hallmark hall of fame (Television program).

Price.

> Hallmark hall of fame. Arthur Miller's The price / a Talent Associates, Norton Simon, inc. production in association with the National Broadcasting Company ; produced with the NBC-TV Network ; Hallmark Cards ; producer, David Susskind ; director, Fielder Cook. United States: NBC, [1971–02–03], c1970.

> **Cast:** Starred George C. Scott as Victor Franz; co-starred Barry Sullivan as Walter Franz; David Burns as Gregory Solomon and Colleen Dewhurst as Esther Franz.

> **Credits:** Associate producer, Alan Shayne. Art director, John Clements. Costumes, Ann Roth; assistant to the director, Enid Roth. Lighting director, Jim Boyers; unit manager, Albert Tolley. Floor manager, John Linton; production assistant, Mary Dalison. Production secretary, Pamela Susskind. Music composed by Arthur Rubinstein; music produced by Score Productions Inc. Recorded at Intertel Colour Television Ltd. Studios, England.

> Play; anthology.

> "Adapted by Arthur Miller from his own play"– Television drama series programming, 1959–1975 / Larry James Gianakos.

> Originally broadcast Wednesday evening, February 3, 1971, 7:30 to 9:00 p.m., according to Television drama series programming, 1959–1975 / Larry James Gianakos.

> Original format: videotape.

Copyright notice on film: c1970 Talent Associates-Norton Simon, Inc.

Commercials: Hallmark Valentine's Day cards—Hallmark Valentine's Day cards—Hallmark party accessories—Hallmark writing instruments—Hallmark writing papers—Hallmark Cards—Hallmark Cards.

Cataloged April 22, 1988, jm; rev. April 13, 2001, my; rev. September 19, 2005, my.

Genre(s)/Form(s): Plays.

Anthologies.

Credits heading(s): Miller, Arthur, 1915- Price.

Susskind, David, 1920- production

Cook, Fielder, 1923- direction

Shayne, Alan. production

Clements, John. production design

Roth, Ann. production design

Rubinstein, Artur, 1887- music

Scott, George C., 1927- cast

Sullivan, Barry, 1912- cast

Burns, David, 1902–1971. cast

Dewhurst, Colleen. cast

Talent Associates.

Norton Simon Inc.

National Broadcasting Company, inc.

NBC Television Network.

Hallmark Cards, Inc.

Commercials. Hallmark.

Varying form of title: Price.

Arthur Miller's the price.

BBID (expression): 46411

Database: Film and Television Archive

Location: NON-CIRCULATING RESEARCH AND STUDY
CENTER COPY

Inventory Number: VA455 T

Collection: HHF Hallmark Collection

TV Television Collection

Format: 1 videocassette of 1 (VHS) (90 min.) : sd., b&w ; 1/2 in.

Reproduction: Los Angeles, Calif.: UCLA Film and Television
Archive, 1985. Reproduced from 16 mm. kinescope
(T3479). Reproduction for preservation purposes
permitted and funded by Hallmark.

Notes: NOTES: Copy added from inventory record without
viewing or inspection. OLD INVENTORY NUMBER:
T21554.

Added copy, April 22, 1988, jm; rev. October 24, 2003,
my; rev. September 19, 2005, my.

HLDID (manifestation): 78029

Location: NON-CIRCULATING RESEARCH AND STUDY
CENTER COPY

Inventory Number: VA13023 T

Collection: TV Television Collection

Format: 1 videocassette of 1 (VHS) (75 min.) : sd., col. ; 1/2 in.

Condition: Commercials: Blacks have been pulled up. Version
dubbed at NBC on September 6, 1971 expressly for
submission to the Peabody Awards; all references to
Hallmark were deleted as were the Hallmark
commercials.

Reproduction: Los Angeles, Calif.: UCLA Film and Television
Archive, March, 1996. Reproduced by UCLA Film and
Television Archive at KTLA from 3/4 in.
videocassettes (T56070). Reproduction for
preservation purposes permitted by Hallmark.

Notes: Added copy by unknown person on unknown date; rev.
September 19, 2005, my.

HLDID (manifestation): 78032

Location: Non-circulating Preservation Vault archival copy

Inventory Number: XVB57 T

Collection: TV Television Collection

Format: 1 videocassette of 1 (Betacam) (75 min.) : sd., col. ; 1/2 in.

Condition: Commercials: Blacks have been pulled up. Version dubbed at NBC on September 6, 1971 expressly for submission to the Peabody Awards; all references to Hallmark were deleted as were the Hallmark commercials.

Reproduction: Los Angeles, Calif.: UCLA Film and Television Archive, March, 1996. Reproduced by UCLA Film and Television Archive at KTLA from D2 videocassette (XVE827 T). Reproduction for preservation purposes permitted by Hallmark.

Notes: Added copy by unknown person on unknown date; rev. September 19, 2005, my.

HLDID (manifestation): 78034

Location: Non-circulating Preservation Vault archival copy

Inventory Number: XVE828 T

Collection: TV Television Collection

Format: 1 videoreel of 1 (Type C) (110 min.) : sd., col. ; 1 in.

Condition: Commercials: Blacks have been pulled up. Version dubbed at NBC on September 6, 1971 expressly for submission to the Peabody Awards; all references to Hallmark were deleted as were the Hallmark commercials.

Reproduction: Los Angeles, Calif.: UCLA Film and Television Archive, March, 1996. Reproduced by UCLA Film and Television Archive at KTLA from D2 videocassette (XVE827 T). Reproduction for preservation purposes permitted by Hallmark.

Notes: Added copy by unknown person on unknown date; rev. September 19, 2005, my.

HLDID (manifestation): 78035

Location: Non-circulating Preservation Vault archival copy

Inventory Number: XVE827 T

Collection: TV Television Collection

Format: 1 videocassette of 1 (75 min.) : sd., col. ; D2.

Condition: Commercials: Blacks have been pulled up. Version dubbed at NBC on September 6, 1971 expressly for submission to the Peabody Awards; all references to Hallmark were deleted as were the Hallmark commercials.

Reproduction: Los Angeles, Calif.: UCLA Film and Television Archive, March, 1996. Reproduced by UCLA Film and Television Archive at KTLA from 2 in. videoreel supplied by donor no. 1622. Reproduction for preservation purposes permitted by Hallmark.

Notes: Added copy by unknown person on unknown date; rev. September 19, 2005, my.

HLDID (manifestation): 78036

Location: Non-circulating Preservation Vault archival copy

Inventory Number: T84356

Collection: TV Television Collection

Format: 1 videocassette of 1 (Digital Betacam) (74 min.) : sd., col. ; 1/2 in.

Condition: Commercials: Blacks have been pulled up. Version dubbed at NBC on September 6, 1971 expressly for submission to the Peabody Awards; all references to Hallmark were deleted as were the Hallmark commercials.

Reproduction: Los Angeles, Calif.: UCLA Film and Television Archive, March 6, 2001. Reproduced at KTLA from D2 videocassette (XVE827 T). Reproduction for preservation purposes permitted by Hallmark.

Notes: LOCATION: PRES. VAULT.

Added copy, June 26, 2001, jj; rev. September 19, 2005, my.

HLDID (manifestation): 244594

Location:	Non-circulating SRLF archival copy
Inventory Number:	T23202
Collection:	HHF Hallmark Collection
	TV Television Collection
Format:	2 videocassettes of 2 (90 min.) : sd., b&w ; 3/4 in.
Reproduction:	Los Angeles, Calif.: UCLA Film and Television Archive, 1985. Reproduced from 16 mm. kinescope (T3479). Reproduction for preservation purposes permitted and funded by Hallmark.
Notes:	NOTES: "3/4VT 5012"–Inventory card.
	Cataloged April 22, 1988, jm; rev. April 13, 2001, my; rev. September 19, 2005, my.
HLDID (manifestation):	78030

Location:	Non-circulating SRLF archival copy
Inventory Number:	T56070
Collection:	TV Television Collection
Format:	2 videocassettes of 2 (75 min.) : sd., col. ; 3/4 in.
Condition:	Commercials: Blacks have been pulled up. Version dubbed at NBC on September 6, 1971 expressly for submission to the Peabody Awards; all references to Hallmark were deleted as were the Hallmark commercials.
Reproduction:	Los Angeles, Calif.: UCLA Film and Television Archive, March, 1996. Reproduced by UCLA Film and Television Archive at KTLA from D2 videocassette (XVE827 T). Reproduction for preservation purposes permitted by Hallmark.
Notes:	Added copy by unknown person at unknown date; rev. September 19, 2005, my.
HLDID (manifestation):	78033

Location: Non-circulating SRLF archival copy

Inventory Number: T3479

Collection: HHF Hallmark Collection

TV Television Collection

Format: 2 reels of 2 (90 min.) (ca. 3200 ft.) : opt sd., b&w ; 16 mm. kinescope.

Notes: NOTES: Copy added from inventory record without viewing or inspection. Former Archive inventory no.: H38.

LOCATION: A2-303-2.

Added copy, April 22, 1988, jm; rev. September 19, 2005, my.

HLDID (manifestation): 78031

Resources for Sample Metadata Records

There are a few resources where sample metadata or cataloging records from a wide variety of organizations can be reviewed for guidance.

Martin, Abigail Leab, ed. *AMIA Compendium of Moving Image Cataloging Practice.* Chicago: Society of American Archivists, 2001. A snapshot in time of the cataloging practices of 27 diverse institutions, including historical societies, university archives, broadcast organizations, museums, and subject-specialized collections. The collections include television, film, and video and utilize both MARC and non-MARC cataloging. This was a project of the Cataloging Committee of the Association of Moving Image Archivists (AMIA), an organization of individuals working with film and broadcasting collections. The introduction and appendices that include contributors' sample cataloging records and cataloging guidelines are available on the AMIA website at: www.amianet.org/publication/resources/cataloging/compendium/appendixE.html.

Moving Image Collections (MIC) (http://mic.imtc.gatech.edu/index.php). This is a union catalog of moving image collections primarily held in the United States and is a joint project of the Library of Congress and the Association of Moving Image Archivists (AMIA). Contributors submit records mapped to the MIC data elements. Records can be submitted in MARC or MPEG7 and can be displayed in several formats: MIC, XML, MARC, and MPEG7. This site is a useful reference to view how data records appear in these different formats. To view sample records from select contributors, visit http://web.archive.org/web/20040220112910/mic.rutgers.edu/MIC/UC/UC_UnionCatalog.php. To see how MIC maps its data elements to MARC and MPEG7 (maps are at the bottom of the page), visit http://mic.imtc.gatech.edu/catalogers_portal/cat_unicatlg.htm.

Appendix 2 Extracts from SMPTE Documents

This appendix presents extracts from the Society of Motion Picture and Television Engineer's Metadata Dictionary RP210 (or Register of Metadata Elements) as current in October 2005 and from Descriptive Metadata Scheme 1 (SMPTE380M). Copies of SMPTE's Standards and Recommended Practices are available via the society's website at www.smpte.org.

The extract in Figure A2.1, from the interpretive section of the dictionary, demonstrates the node and leaf structure of the register. It also shows examples of the unique key used for each element: the name, definition, datatype, and length of the element's value (in bytes).

The register lists more than 1,700 entries, and it is continually being updated. At the time of this writing, unique eXtensible Mark-up Language (XML) tags are in the standardization ballot process to add to the register, and online access is being developed. The latest published version of the register can be found on the SMPTE's Registration Authority's Metadata Registry website at: www.smpte-ra.org/mdd/index.html. The structure of the register is specified in standard SMPTE335.

Figure A2.2 is an extract from the SMPTE Descriptive Metadata Scheme 1 (DMS-1), showing how metadata elements are arranged into groups. The extract shown is from the production framework.

SMPTE Metadata Dictionary

Version 8

final, August 10th, 2004

Please read in conjunction with the cover sheet of this workbook

Note: 8
457
1363

Dictionary Version at Introduction	Node or Leaf	SMPTE Designator	SMPTE Item	Data Element Name	Data Element Definition	Type	Value Length	Value Range
1	Node	06.0E.2B.34.01.01.01.01	03.01.03.00.00.00.00.00	Fundamental Dimensions	Information about the four basic indefinables of natural philosophy			
1	Node	06.0E.2B.34.01.01.01.01	03.01.03.01.00.00.00.00	Length	Descriptive information about length (Default is Metric system, metres)			
1	Leaf	06.0E.2B.34.01.01.01.01	03.01.03.01.01.00.00.00	Length System	Metric, Imperial etc	ISO/IEC 646:1991 - ISO 7-Bit Coded Character Set	4 chars max	
1	Leaf	06.0E.2B.34.01.01.01.01	03.01.03.01.02.00.00.00	Length Units	Units of measurements of length and distance (feet, metres etc)	ISO/IEC 646:1991 - ISO 7-Bit Coded Character Set	4 chars max	
1	Node	06.0E.2B.34.01.01.01.01	03.01.03.02.00.00.00.00	Angles	Descriptive information about Angles (Default is Degrees)			
1	Leaf	06.0E.2B.34.01.01.01.01	03.01.03.02.01.00.00.00	Angular Unit	Degrees, Radians, Grads etc	ISO/IEC 646:1991 - ISO 7-Bit Coded Character Set	4 chars max	
1	Node	06.0E.2B.34.01.01.01.01	03.01.03.03.00.00.00.00	Time	Descriptive information about Time (Default is UTC system)			
1	Leaf	06.0E.2B.34.01.01.01.01	03.01.03.03.01.00.00.00	Time system offset	Time offset from UTC (Signed hours and minutes, colon delineated) (Default is undefined). Positive is East of UMT, negative is West of UMT	ISO/IEC 646:1991 - ISO 7-Bit Coded Character Set	6 chars max	+13hours/-12hours
1	Leaf	06.0E.2B.34.01.01.01.01	03.01.03.03.02.00.00.00	Time Units	Frames, seconds, minutes etc. (Default is seconds)	ISO/IEC 646:1991 - ISO 7-Bit Coded Character Set	4 chars max	
3	Leaf	06.0E.2B.34.01.01.01.03	03.01.03.03.03.00.00.00	Timing Bias Correction	Correction in seconds to be applied to timing metadata or essence title.	Floating Point	4 byte	
3	Leaf	06.0E.2B.34.01.01.01.03	03.01.03.03.04.00.00.00	Description of Timing Bias Correction	Description of the timing bias computation, reason, etc.	ISO/IEC 646:1991 - ISO 7-Bit Coded Character Set	40 bytes max	
1	Node	06.0E.2B.34.01.01.01.01	03.01.03.04.00.00.00.00	Mass	Descriptive information about Mass (Default is Metric system, Kilograms)			
1	Leaf	06.0E.2B.34.01.01.01.01	03.01.03.05.00.00.00.00	Energy	Descriptive information about Energy (Default is Joule)			
1	Node	06.0E.2B.34.01.01.01.01	03.02.00.00.00.00.00.00	Descriptive - Human Assigned	Descriptor (Human Assigned) relating to analysis of the content			
1	Node	06.0E.2B.34.01.01.01.01	03.02.01.00.00.00.00.00	Categorisation	Analytical categorization of the content			
1	Node	06.0E.2B.34.01.01.01.01	03.02.01.01.00.00.00.00	Content Classification	Content classification			
1	Leaf	06.0E.2B.34.01.01.01.01	03.02.01.01.01.00.00.00	Content Coding System	The system of coding for programme classification e.g. Escort 2.4	ISO/IEC 646:1991 - ISO 7-Bit Coded Character Set	31 bytes max	
1	Leaf	06.0E.2B.34.01.01.01.01	03.02.01.02.00.00.00.00	Programme Type	Type of programme (e.g., cartoon, film,...)	ISO/IEC 646:1991 - ISO 7-Bit Coded Character Set	32 bytes max	
1	Leaf	06.0E.2B.34.01.01.01.01	03.02.01.02.01.00.00.00	Genre	Programme genre (e.g. entertainment, current affairs magazine, Italo Western,...)	ISO/IEC 646:1991 - ISO 7-Bit Coded Character Set	32 bytes max	
3	Leaf	06.0E.2B.34.01.01.01.03	03.02.01.04.00.00.00.00	Genre	Programme genre (e.g. entertainment, current affairs magazine, Italo Western,...)	16 bit Unicode String	64 bytes max	
1	Leaf	06.0E.2B.34.01.01.01.01	03.02.01.04.01.00.00.00	Target Audience	Target audience (e.g., children, 17 to 32, elderly, ...)	ISO/IEC 646:1991 - ISO 7-Bit Coded Character Set	32 bytes max	
3	Leaf	06.0E.2B.34.01.01.01.03	03.02.01.04.01.00.00.00	Target Audience	Target audience (e.g., children, 17 to 32, elderly, ...)	16 bit Unicode String	Variable	
3	Leaf	06.0E.2B.34.01.01.01.03	03.02.01.10.00.00.00.00	Programme material classification Code	The resulting delineated classification code from the classification system	ISO/IEC 646:1991 - ISO 7-Bit Coded Character Set	16 bytes max	
1	Node	06.0E.2B.34.01.01.01.01	03.02.02.01.00.00.00.00	Cataloguing and Indexing	Archival analysis of the essence metadata			
1	Leaf	06.0E.2B.34.01.01.01.01	03.02.02.01.00.00.00.00	Status of Catalogue Data	The current status of the catalogue as a freeform text string	ISO/IEC 646:1991 - ISO 7-Bit Coded Character Set	127 bytes max	
1	Leaf	06.0E.2B.34.01.01.01.01	03.02.02.02.00.00.00.00	Thesaurus Name	The name of a specialised vocabulary of selected words or concepts for a particular field, e.g. cataloguing, indexing or thesaurus system	ISO/IEC 646:1991 - ISO 7-Bit Coded Character Set	32 bytes max	
4	Leaf	06.0E.2B.34.01.01.01.04	03.02.02.02.01.00.00.00	Thesaurus Name	The name of a specialised vocabulary of selected words or concepts for a particular field, e.g. cataloguing, indexing or thesaurus system	16 bit Unicode String	Variable	
1	Leaf	06.0E.2B.34.01.01.01.01	03.02.02.03.00.00.00.00	Theme	The category of the Theme of the content	ISO/IEC 646:1991 - ISO 7-Bit Coded Character Set	32 bytes max	
3	Leaf	06.0E.2B.34.01.01.01.03	03.02.02.03.01.00.00.00	Theme	The category of the Theme of the content	16 bit Unicode String	Variable	
1	Leaf	06.0E.2B.34.01.01.01.01	03.02.02.04.00.00.00.00	Content Classification	The value of the content classification as a (possibly subdivided) alphanumeric string	ISO/IEC 646:1991 - ISO 7-Bit Coded Character Set	127 bytes max	
1	Leaf	06.0E.2B.34.01.01.01.01	03.02.01.02.04.00.00.00	Subject	The Subject being indexed expressed as a Name.	ISO/IEC 646:1991 - ISO 7-Bit Coded Character Set	32 bytes max	
3	Leaf	06.0E.2B.34.01.01.01.03	03.02.01.02.04.02.00.00	Subject	The Subject being indexed expressed as a Name.	16 bit Unicode String	64 bytes max	
1	Leaf	06.0E.2B.34.01.01.01.01	03.02.02.05.00.00.00.00	Key Words	Words or phrases summarizing an aspect of the data set.	ISO/IEC 646:1991 - ISO 7-Bit Coded Character Set	127 bytes max	
3	Leaf	06.0E.2B.34.01.01.01.03	03.02.01.02.05.01.00.00	Key Words	Words or phrases summarizing an aspect of the data set.	16 bit Unicode String	Variable	
1	Leaf	06.0E.2B.34.01.01.01.01	03.02.02.06.00.00.00.00	Key Frames	Freeform textual reference to a key frame of video in the data set	ISO/IEC 646:1991 - ISO 7-Bit Coded Character Set	127 bytes max	
1	Leaf	06.0E.2B.34.01.01.01.01	03.02.02.07.00.00.00.00	Key Sounds	Freeform textual reference to a key piece of data in the data set	ISO/IEC 646:1991 - ISO 7-Bit Coded Character Set	127 bytes max	

Figure A2.1. An extract from the SMPTE Metadata Dictionary, version 8 (October 2005).

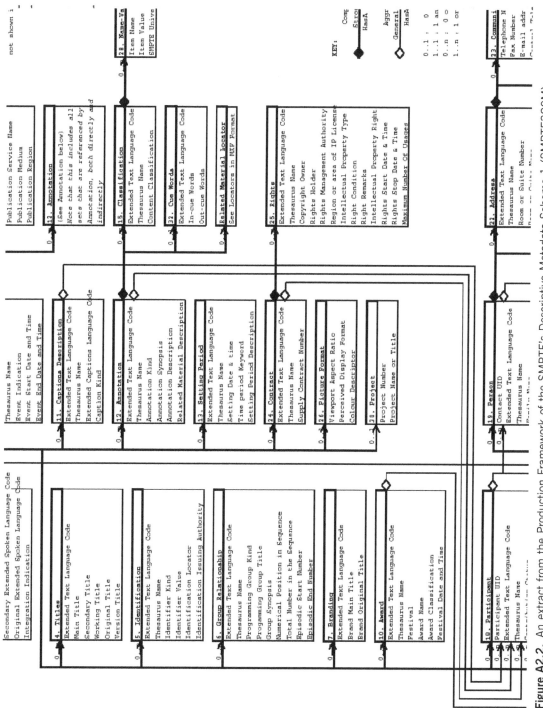

Figure A2.2. An extract from the Production Framework of the SMPTE's Descriptive Metadata Scheme 1 (SMPTE380M).

DMS-1 is part of the Material eXchange Format suite of documents and builds on the underlying structure of the MXF file. Therefore, metadata used in structuring the file itself (for example, TV line standards) is not repeated in DMS-1.

Index

A

AACR2 (Anglo-American Cataloguing Rules, 2nd edition, 2002 revision), 9, 53–54

AAF (Advanced Authoring Format), 65–66

Acquisition information, 111

Additional data essence, 90

Administrative metadata, 21

ADSL (asymmetric digital subscriber line) broadband, 89

Advanced Authoring Format (AAF), 65–66

Advanced Television Systems Committee (ATSC), 80, 87

Agents, software, 98

Aggregated metadata, 96

American Association of Advertising Industries, 80

American Chemical Society, 80

AMIA (Association of Moving Image Archivists), 130

AMIA Compendium of Moving Image Cataloging Practice, 130

AMIM2 (Archival Moving Image Materials, Version 2), 9, 54

Anglo-American Cataloguing Rules, 2nd edition, 2002 revision (AACR2), 9, 53–54

Archival metadata, 28

Archival Moving Image Materials, Version 2 (AMIM2), 9, 54

Archival research, 11

Archival standards, 52–53

    Independent Media Arts Preservation (IMAP), 53

    International Federation of Television Archives (FIAT/IFTA), 52

Archives, 21, 28

Archivists, 22, 72

Association of Moving Image Archivists (AMIA), 130

Asymmetric digital subscriber line (ADSL) broadband, 89

Atmosphere field, TV-Anytime program, 101

ATSC (Advanced Television Systems Committee), 80, 87

Attractors, 95, 98–101

Audio and video information, 104

AudioCoding element, 104

Audiovisual (AV) media files, 70

Authenticity in metadata, 73–74

Automatic authentication, 70

Automatic capture, 65–66

Automatic metadata-generation, 63, 67

Automatic system alert, 28

Automatic text-based indexing, 6

AV (audiovisual) media files, 70

Awards, 98

B

BBC (British Broadcasting Corporation) standard media exchange framework, 50

BMEF (Broadcast Metadata Exchange Format), 44

Book-marking systems, 6

"Box level" descriptions, 112

British Broadcasting Corporation (BBC) standard media exchange framework, 50

Broadband Internet connections, 93

Broadcast industry standards, 41–50

  BBC Standard Media Exchange Framework, 50

  Corporation for Public Broadcasting PBCore, 49

  European Broadcasting Union P/Meta, 43–44

  Institut für Rundfunktechnik GmbH (IRT), 44

  Motion Picture Experts Group MPEG-21, 47–49

  Motion Picture Experts Group MPEG-7, 44–47

  Society of Motion Picture and Television Engineers (SMPTE), 41–43

Broadcast Metadata Exchange Format (BMEF), 44

Broadcasting Organisation Facility Codes, 83

Business metadata, 21

Business ownership of metadata, 69–70

C

Cable Labs OpenCable Applications Platform (OCAP), 89

Capturing metadata, 64–67, 70, 84

Catalogers, 7, 20, 111, 113

Cataloging, 6, 69

cIDF (Content ID Forum), 80, 87

Clip information, 43

CNN digital library system, 118–122

CNRI (Corporation for National Research Initiatives), 80, 87–88

Commercial On Demand services, 105

Commercials, 105

Commissioners, 25

Commissioning process, 23

Complex objects, 40–41

Computer data files, 4

Consumer metadata

  broadcast and Internet content connector, 93–94

  and Internet, 91–93

  marketing, 102–105

  metadata elements, 97–101

    attractors, 98–101

    Content Reference ID (CRID), 97–98

  and program-making metadata, 64

  TV-Anytime metadata data model, 95–97

    content creation, 95

    content publishing, 95

    content selection, 97

    location resolution, 97

    metadata aggregation, 96

    metadata editing, 95–96

    metadata publishing, 96

Consumer relevance, identifiers with production to, 86–88

  Advanced Television Systems Committee (ATSC), 87

  Content ID Forum (cIDF), 87

  Corporation for National Research Initiatives (CNRI), 87–88

  Digital Video Broadcasting Project (DVB), 86–87

  Internet Assigned Numbers Authority (IANA), 87

  TV-Anytime Forum, 87

Content alert field, TV-Anytime program, 101

Content creation, TV-Anytime metadata data model, 95

Content field, TV-Anytime program classification, 101

Content ID Forum (cIDF), 80, 87

Content management description tools, 47

Content organization description tools, 47

Content ownership, 68–69

Content publishing process, 95

Content publishing, TV-Anytime metadata data model, 95

Content reference identifier (CRID), 87, 95, 97–98, 101

Content selection process, 96–97

Controlled vocabularies, 54–55, 81

Copyright, 87, 99

Corporation for National Research Initiatives (CNRI), 80, 87–88

Corporation for Public Broadcasting (CPB), 38, 49

CPB (Corporation for Public Broadcasting), 38, 49
Creation workflow, 67
CRID (content reference identifier), 87, 95, 97–98, 101
Current affairs programs and documentaries, 108–109

D
DAM (digital asset management system), 54, 67
Data, 7–10
    rules, 8–9
    structure or schema, 8
    values, 9–10
Data modeling, 38
Datatypes Registries, 81
DDL (description definition language), MPEG-7, 46
Defining metadata
    broadcasting technologies relationships, 4–5
    data, 7–10
        rules, 8–9
        structure or schema, 8
        values, 9–10
    data handling relationships, 5–6
    details, 10–11
    information science relationships, 6–7
    libraries, 11–14
        broadcast entertainment, 12–13
        broadcast news, 12
        film studios, 11–12
        TV-anytime forum, 13–14
    locating metadata, 14–18
    managing knowledge during production, 10
    myths and facts, 2–3
    perceptions, 3–4
Description definition language (DDL), MPEG-7, 46
Description schemes (DS), 47
Descriptive elements, 51
Descriptive metadata, 19–20
Descriptive Metadata Scheme-1 (DMS-1), 43, 60, 131
Descriptors, 45, 47
Desktop production, 70–71

Digital asset management system (DAM), 54, 67
Digital rights management (DRM), 21
Digital subscriber line (DSL) connections, 91
Digital Video Broadcasting Project (DVB), 80, 86–87
Digital Video Broadcasting's Multimedia Home Platform (DVB-MHP), 89
Digital video recorder (DVR), 105
DMS-1 (Descriptive Metadata Scheme-1), 43, 60, 131
DOI (International Digital Object Identifier) Foundation, 79, 82
Domain names, 87
Downloadable fonts, 90
Downloaded metadata, 93
DRM (digital rights management), 21
DS (description schemes), 47
DSL (digital subscriber line) connections, 91
Dublin Core metadata initiative, 38, 42, 49, 50–51
DVB (Digital Video Broadcasting Project), 80, 86–87
DVB-MHP (Digital Video Broadcasting's Multimedia Home Platform), 89
DVR (digital video recorder), 105

E
EAD (Encoded Archival Description), 112
ECG (electronic content guide), 13, 89, 91, 93
Edit decision list (EDL), 27
Editing metadata, TV-Anytime metadata data model, 95–96
EDL (edit decision list), 27
Electronic content guide (ECG), 13, 89, 91, 93
Electronic program guide (EPG), 89, 91, 98
Electronic signal, 4
Encoded Archival Description (EAD), 112
Encoding schemes, 37, 59
End-to-end production environment, 10
EPG (electronic program guide), 89, 91, 98
Essence, 3, 77
European Broadcasting Union, 43–44, 79, 83
European Commission research program, 94
European Telecommunications Standards Institute, 80
eXtensible Mark-up Language (XML), 37, 49, 59, 75, 77, 83, 131

F

FIAT/IFTA (International Federation of Television Archives), 52
Field list format, 118
File exchange standards, 18
File formats, 65
File information, 104–105
Fixed/static metadata, 15
Fonts, downloadable, 90
Footage.net, 12
Format field, TV-Anytime program, 100
Frame-bounded metadata, 16
Functional Requirements for Bibliographic Records (FRBR), 40

G

Genre, 19, 20, 57, 100
Global database structures, 103
Global exchange standards, 15
Groups Register, SMPTE, 42

H

House workflow management system, 95

I

IANA (Internet Assigned Numbers Authority), 80, 87
Identification fields, 52
Identification metadata, 20
Identifiers and identification
  consumer relevance, 86–88
    Advanced Television Systems Committee (ATSC), 87
    Content ID Forum (CIDF), 87
    Corporation for National Research Initiatives (CNRI), 87–88
    Digital Video Broadcasting Project (DVB), 86–87
    Internet Assigned Numbers Authority (IANA), 87
    TV-Anytime Forum, 87
  registered identifiers, 78–83
    international registration authorities, 78–81
    program production relevance, 81–83

unregistered identifiers, 84–86
  Unique Material Identifier (UMID), 84–85
  Universal Unique Identifier (UUID), 85–86
IEEE (Institution of Electrical and Electronic Engineers), 79, 82
IEEE device identifier, 84
IETF (Internet Engineering Task Force), 79, 83
IFLA (International Federation of Library Associations and Institutions), 40, 80
IMAP (Independent Media Arts Preservation), 8, 52–53
Independent Media Arts Preservation (IMAP), 8, 52–53
Instantiation elements, 49
Institut für Rundfunktechnik GmBH (IRT), 44
Institution of Electrical and Electronic Engineers (IEEE), 79, 82
Intellectual property, 40, 49, 66, 68
Intended audience field, TV-Anytime program, 101
Intention field, TV-Anytime program, 100
Interactive digital broadcast services, 29
Interactive metadata requirements, 25
Interactive television (iTV) application developers, 91
Interactive TV programming, 91
International Digital Object Identifier (DOI) Foundation, 79, 82
International Federation of Library Associations and Institutions (IFLA), 40, 80
International Federation of Television Archives (FIAT/IFTA), 52
International Press Telecommunications Council (IPTC), 55–56
International registration authorities, 78–81
International Standard Audio-Visual Number (ISAN), 78, 81, 103
International Standards Organisation (ISO), 79, 81
International Standards Organisation/ International Electrotechnical Commission (ISO/IEC) standard, 44
Internet Assigned Numbers Authority (IANA), 80, 87
Internet Engineering Task Force (IETF), 79, 83
Internet Protocol (IP) address, 87
IP (Internet Protocol) address, 87
IPTC (International Press Telecommunications Council), 55–56

IRT (Institut für Rundfunktechnik GmBH), 44
ISAN (International Standard Audio-Visual
    Number), 78, 81, 103
ISO (International Standards Organisation), 79,
    81
ISO/IEC (International Standards
    Organisation/International Electrotechnical
    Commission) standard, 44
ISO/IEC JTC1/SC29/WG11 (Joint Technical
    Committee1/Sub-Committee 29/Working
    Group11), 44
ITV (interactive television) application
    developers, 91
ITV Association, 80

J
Joint Technical Committee1/Sub-Committee
    29/Working Group11 (ISO/IEC
    JTC1/SC29/WG11), 44

K
Kentucky Educational Television (KET),
    113–115
Key encoding, 100
Key metadata, 12
Key-length-value (KLV) encoding protocol, 37,
    43, 59
Keywords, 110
Kinescope recording, 108
KLV (key-length-value) encoding protocol, 37,
    43, 59
Knowledge management, 66, 67, 71
Knowledge-based indexing system, 6

L
Labels, 43, 77, 81
Language-related information, 99
LCNAF (Library of Congress Name Authority
    File), 10, 56–57, 122
LCSH (Library of Congress Subject Headings),
    10, 57
Legacy data, 109
Legal fields, 52
Legal information ownership, 68–69
Legal metadata, 21

Libraries, 11–14
    broadcast entertainment, 12–13
    broadcast news, 12
    film studios, 11–12
    structure standards, 50–52
        Dublin Core Metadata Initiative, 50–51
        Library of Congress MARC 21, 51–52
    television, 13–14
Library of Congress Name Authority File
    (LCNAF), 10, 56–57, 122
Library of Congress Subject Headings (LCSH),
    10, 57
Library science, 6, 7, 20, 66, 67
Licensing, 11, 12
Live transmitted metadata, 93
Local registration authority, 77
Local television newsfilm, 109–110
Location resolution, 95, 97
Logging of metadata, 26–27
Losing metadata, 72–73
Low-resolution proxy version, 16

M
MAC (medium access control) address, 82
Machine-Readable Cataloguing (MARC), 51,
    51–52, 56, 110, 122–130
Mapping metadata to different systems, 39,
    74–75
MARC (Machine-Readable Cataloguing), 51,
    51–52, 56, 110, 122–130
Marketing, 102–105
Master metadata, 73
Material eXchange Format (MXF), 43, 60, 65, 134
Media asset management systems, 63
Media review information, 99
Media type field, TV-Anytime program, 101
Medium access control (MAC) address, 82
Metadata aggregation, 96
Metadata channel, 91
Metadata creation, 68
Metadata dictionary, 38, 41, 49, 120
Metadata Dictionary, SMPTE RP210, 42, 81,
    131–132
Metadata elements, 31–36, 97–101
    attractors, 98
    Content Reference ID (CRID), 97–98
    creating attractors, 98–101

Metadata manager, 68
Metadata "mixer," 17
Metadata registries, 81
Metadata schemes, 38
Metadata-containing video streams, 74
MIC (Moving Image Collections), 130
Mirror metadata, 73
Modification date, 104
Moving image catalogers, 41
Moving Image Collections (MIC), 130
Moving Image Genre-Form Guide, 10, 57
Moving Picture Experts Group (MPEG), 44
MPEG (Moving Picture Experts Group), 44
MPEG-7, 44–47
MPEG-21 framework, 47–49
MPEG-21 Rights Data Dictionary, 82
Multimedia Content Description Interface, 45
MXF (Material eXchange Format), 43, 60, 65, 134

N
Naming conventions, 72
Narrative summaries, 20
Networking technology, 62, 82
News footage cataloging, 118–122
Newsfilm, 107–108
NewsML, 50
Non-real-time applications, 46
Notional workflow, 23

O
Object record concept, 76
OCAP (Cable Labs OpenCable Applications
    Platform), 89
OCLC (Online Computer Library Center), 52
Off-air recording, 109
On-demand channels, 93
Online catalogs, 7, 111
Online Computer Library Center (OCLC), 52
Online databases, 7
Open standards, 7–8
Origination field, TV-Anytime program, 101
Orphan metadata, 72
Overarching metadata scheme, 75
Ownership of metadata, 67–70
    business ownership, 69–70

legal information and metadata content
    ownership, 68–69
workflow ownership, 67–68

P
Parallel metadata tracks, 18
Parallel storage systems, 15
Parental guidance information, 99
PBCore, 42, 49, 113–118
    Kentucky Educational Television (KET),
        113–114
    Wisconsin Public Television (WPTV),
        116–118
Personal video recorder (PVR), 105
Physical forms, 22
Physical mediums, 111
Plain old telephone system (POTS), 91
P/Meta, 44
POTS (plain old telephone system), 91
"Precise" elements, 39
Preservation metadata, 21–22
Preserving metadata, 110–111
Press industry standards, 50
Program classification, 100, 101
Program makers, 2
Program production relevance, identifiers with,
    81–83
    European Broadcasting Union, 83
    Institution of Electrical & Electronic Engineers
        (IEEE), 82
    International Digital Object Identifier (DOI)
        Foundation, 82
    International Standards Organisation, 81
    Internet Engineering Task Force (IETF), 83
    Society of Motion Picture and Television
        Engineers Registration Authority, 81
Program production workflow, 23
Program-making metadata, 64
Program-making workflow, 38, 74–75
Proxies, 3, 4, 70–71
Public collections, 106–112
    donations by broadcasters, 107–109
        current affairs programs and documentaries,
            108–109
        newsfilm, 107–108
    donations by individuals and production
        companies, 109

metadata added by public archive, 109–111
  adapting legacy metadata, 109–110
  intellectual property, 111
  preserving metadata, 110–111
  tracking history and provenance, 110
off-air recording, 109
public accessibility, 111–112
Publishing content, TV-Anytime metadata data model, 95
Publishing metadata, TV-Anytime metadata data model, 96
PVR (personal video recorder), 105
PVR/DVR devices, 105

R
Radiotelevisione Italiana (RAI), 44
Raw news footage cataloging, 118–122
Real-time applications, 45–46
Recommended Practice 210 (SMPTE RP210), 42, 131–132
Registered identifiers, 78–83
  international registration authorities, 78–81
  program production relevance, 81–83
    European Broadcasting Union, 83
    Institution of Electrical and Electronic Engineers (IEEE), 82
    International Digital Object Identifier (DOI) foundation, 82
    International Standards Organisation, 81
    Internet Engineering Task Force (IETF), 83
    Society of Motion Picture and Television Engineers Registration Authority, 81
Related content, 13
Relevant legacy metadata, 106
Resourcing, 25
Reverse mapping, 39
Rights, *see* Copyright
Rights Data Dictionary, MPEG21, 82
Rights tracking, 15
RP210 (SMPTE), 42, 81, 131–132
Rules standards, 53–54

S
Sample metadata records, 113–130
  entertainment program in MARC, 122–130
  PBCore, 113–118

Kentucky Educational Television (KET), 113–114
Wisconsin Public Television (WPTV), 116–118
raw news footage cataloging: CNN, 118–122
resources for, 130
SAVANT (Synchronised and Scalable Audio Video Content Across NeTworks), 93
Scene changes, 26–27
Scheduled programme description metadata, 103
Schemes, structures, and encoding
  encoding, 59–60
  maintenance, 58
  records, object and item, 40–41
  rules standards, 53–54
    Anglo-American Cataloguing Rules (AACR2), 53–54
    Archival Moving Image Materials, Version 2 (AMIM2), 54
  schemes and structures, 37–40
  structure standards, 41–53
    archival, 52–53
    broadcast industry, 41–50
    library, 50–52
  value standards, 54–57
    controlled vocabularies and thesauri, 54–55
    International Press Telecommunications Council (IPTC), 55–56
    Library of Congress Name Authority File (LCNAF), 56–57
    Library of Congress Subject Headings (LCSH), 57
    Moving Image Genre-Form Guide, 57
Search engines, 6
Segmentation, 95, 99–100
Selecting content, TV-Anytime metadata data model, 97
Self-contained encoding schemes, 59
Service information (SI), 29
Set-top box, 13, 90
Shotlist records, 110
SI (service information), 29
SMEF (Standard Media Exchange Format), 44
SMEF-DM (Standard Media Exchange Framework Data Model), 50
SMPTE (Society of Motion Picture and Television Engineers), 3, 30, 38, 41–43, 131–134
SMPTE Groups Register, 42

SMPTE Metadata Dictionary (RP210), 42, 81, 131–132
SMPTE Metadata Registries, 81
Society of Motion Picture and Television Engineers Registration Authority, 79, 81
Society of Motion Picture and Television Engineers (SMPTE), 3, 30, 38, 41–43, 131–134
Standard Media Exchange Format (SMEF), 44
Standard Media Exchange Framework Data Model (SMEF-DM), 50
Standard metadata groups, 40
Storing metadata, 64–67
Stripped-off metadata, 17
Structure standards, 41–53
   archival, 41–53
      Independent Media Arts Preservation (IMAP), 52–53
      International Federation of Television Archives (FIAT/IFTA), 52
   broadcast industry, 41–50
      BBC Standard Media Exchange Framework, 50
      Corporation for Public Broadcasting PBCore, 49
      European Broadcasting Union P/Meta, 43–44
      Institut für Rundfunktechnik GmbH (IRT), 44
      Motion Picture Experts Group MPEG-21, 47–49
      Motion Picture Experts Group MPEG-7, 44–47
      Society of Motion Picture and Television Engineers (SMPTE), 41–43
   library, 50–52
      Dublin Core metadata initiative, 50–51
      Library of Congress MARC 21, 51–52
   press industry, 50
Synchronised and Scalable Audio Video Content Across NeTworks (SAVANT), 93
Synchronization, 18, 74

T
Tape library, 11
Tape recording, 108
Technical metadata, 14, 25

Technology change, impact of, 61–75
   authenticity in metadata, 73–74
   capturing and storing metadata, 64–67
   desktop production, 70–71
   losing metadata, 72–73
   mapping metadata to different systems, 74–75
   ownership of metadata, 67–70
      business ownership, 69–70
      legal information and metadata content ownership, 68–69
      workflow ownership, 67–68
Textual description, 100
Thesauri, 54–55
Time-code metadata, 64
Tracking file components, 86
Transmission information, 92
TV-Anytime (TVA) forum, 13, 80, 87, 89, 92, 94
TV-Anytime CRID, 103
TV-Anytime metadata data model, 95–97
   content creation, 95
   content publishing, 95
   content selection, 97
   location resolution, 97
   metadata aggregation, 96
   metadata editing, 95–96
   metadata publishing, 96
Types of metadata, 19–22
   administrative, 21
   descriptive, 19–20
   preservation, 21–22

U
UCLA (University of California Los Angeles) Film and Television Archive, 107, 122
U-matic videocassettes, 107, 108
UMID (Unique Material Identifier), 70, 84–85
Uniform resource identifier (URI), 83
Unique Material Identifier (UMID), 70, 84–85
Universal Unique Identifier (UUID), 85–86
University of California Los Angeles (UCLA) Film and Television Archive, 107, 122
University of Georgia Peabody Awards Archive, 107
Unregistered identifiers, 77, 78, 84–86
   Unique Material Identifier (UMID), 84–85
   Universal Unique Identifier (UUID), 85–86

URI (uniform resource identifier), 83
UUID (Universal Unique Identifier), 85–86

V
Value standards, 54–57
    controlled vocabularies and thesauri, 54–55
    International Press Telecommunications
        Council (IPTC), 55–56
    Library of Congress Name Authority File
        (LCNAF), 56–57
    Library of Congress Subject Headings (LCSH),
        57
    Moving Image Genre-Form Guide, 57
Version International Standard Audio-Visual
    Number (V-ISAN), 81
Video conferencing, 90
Videophone, 90
V-ISAN (Version International Standard
    Audio-Visual Number), 79
VisualCoding element, 104

Vocabularies, controlled, 54–55, 81
Vocabulary register, 42

W
Web content developers, 11
Wisconsin Public Television (WPTV), 113,
    116–118
Workflow, 22–36
    program production and publication,
        22–29
    program publication and consumption,
        30–36
Workflow ownership, 67–68
WPTV (Wisconsin Public Television), 113,
    116–118

X
XML (eXtensible Mark-up Language), 37, 49, 59,
    75, 77, 83, 131

Printed and bound by CPI Group (UK) Ltd, Croydon, CR0 4YY
08/06/2025
01896999-0018